CW00819873

Improving
Personal Effectiveness
for
Managers in
Schools

James Johnston

Published by Network Educational Press Ltd.
PO Box 635
Stafford
ST16 1BF

First Published 1999
© James Johnston 1999

ISBN 1 85539 049 3

Series Editor - Tim Brighouse
Edited by Chris Griffin
Design & layout by
Neil Hawkins of Devine Design
Cover & additional illustrations by Darren Weaver

Printed in Great Britain by
Redwood Books, Trowbridge, Wilts.

Acknowledgements

Many of the techniques described in the book are drawn from the
discipline of *Neuro-Linguistic Programming* (NLP) and I can, therefore,
claim no credit for them. I have included at the end of the book
a range of suggestions for further reading which include a number
of key texts on NLP. I recommend a recognised programme of
training in NLP to any reader who wishes to develop further in this area.

I am particularly indebted to John Seymour of John Seymour Associates
for introducing me so effectively to many of the NLP techniques
described in this book. I would also like to acknowledge the
part played by Chris Lindup (Headteacher, Merrywood School, Bristol),
Isobel Clarke and Anne Papathomas in helping me develop
my ideas and skills in this area. Barbara Teale was kind enough
to read the draft manuscript of this book and to make a
number of helpful suggestions for which I am grateful to her.

Jim Johnston
January, 1999

Foreword

A teacher's task is much more ambitious than it used to be and demands a focus on the subtleties of teaching and learning and on the emerging knowledge of school improvement.

This is what this series is about.

Teaching can be a very lonely activity. The time honoured practice of a single teacher working alone in the classroom is still the norm; yet to operate alone is, in the end to become isolated and impoverished. This series addresses two issues – the need to focus on practical and useful ideas connected with teaching and learning and the wish thereby to provide some sort of an antidote to the loneliness of the long distance teacher who is daily berated by an anxious society.

Teachers flourish best when, in key stage teams or departments (or more rarely whole schools), their talk is predominantly about teaching and learning and where, unconnected with appraisal, they are privileged to observe each other teach; to plan and review their work together; and to practise the habit of learning from each other new teaching techniques. But how does this state of affairs arise? Is it to do with the way staffrooms are physically organised so that the walls bear testimony to interesting articles and in the corner there is a dedicated computer tuned to 'conferences' about SEN, school improvement, the teaching of English etc., and whether, in consequence, the teacher leaning over the shoulder of the enthusiastic IT colleagues sees the promise of interesting practice elsewhere? Has the primary school cracked it when it organises successive staff meetings in different classrooms and invites the 'host' teacher to start the meeting with a 15 minute exposition of their classroom organisation and management? Or is it the same staff sharing, on a rota basis, a slot on successive staff meeting agenda when each in turn reviews a new book they have used with their class? And what of the whole school which now uses 'active' and 'passive' concerts of carefully chosen music as part of their accelerated learning techniques?

It is of course well understood that excellent teachers feel threatened when first they are observed. Hence the epidemic of trauma associated with OFSTED. The constant observation of the teacher in training seems like that of the learner driver. Once you have passed your test and can drive unaccompanied, you do. You often make lots of mistakes and sometimes get into bad habits. Woe betide, however, the back seat driver who tells you so. In the same way the new teacher quickly loses the habit of observing others and being observed. So how do we get a confident, mutual observation debate going? One school I know found a simple and therefore brilliant solution. The Head of the History Department asked that a young colleague plan lessons for her – the Head of Department – to teach. This lesson she then taught, and was observed by the young colleague. There was subsequent discussion, in which the young teacher asked,

> *"Why did you divert the question and answer session I had planned?"*
> *and was answered by,*
> *"Because I could see that I needed to arrest the attention of the group by the window with some "hands-on" role play, etc."*

This lasted an hour and led to a once-a-term repeat discussion which, in the end, was adopted by the whole school. The whole school subsequently changed the pattern of its meetings to consolidate extended debate about teaching and learning. The two teachers claimed that because one planned and the other taught both were implicated but neither alone was responsible or felt 'got at'.

So there are practices which are both practical and more likely to make teaching a rewarding and successful activity. They can, as it were, increase the likelihood of a teacher surprising the pupils into understanding or doing something they did not think they could do rather than simply entertaining them or worse still occupying them. There are ways of helping teachers judge the best method of getting pupil expectation just ahead of self-esteem.

This series focuses on straightforward interventions which individual schools and teachers use to make life more rewarding for themselves and those they teach. Teachers deserve nothing less, for they are the architects of tomorrow's society, and society's ambition for what they achieve increases as each year passes.

Professor Tim Brighouse.

Contents

Introduction   7

Part One

    Section One   **Setting Personal Goals for Success**   9

    Section Two   **Effective Time Management**   19

    Section Three   **Dealing with the Pressures of Leading**   33
                 and Managing in a School

Part Two

    Section Four   **Improving your Communication Skills**   45

    Section Five   **Turning Language to your Advantage**   57

    Section Six   **Resolving Differences Effectively**   71

Conclusion   83

Introduction

Improving Personal Effectiveness

There is only one corner of the Universe you can be certain of improving; and that is your own self.

Aldous Huxley

This is a book about school improvement. It is mainly concerned with bringing about improvement by enhancing the personal effectiveness of leaders and managers in schools.

There has been a great deal of change in Education in the past ten years. The 1988 Education Reform Act; the advent of the National Curriculum; the increasing devolution of responsibility to schools through Local Management of Schools; and requirements such as the National Professional Qualifications for Headteachers (and indeed for subject leaders) have all placed new demands on school teachers and managers.

Traditional roles and responsibilities for heads, deputy heads and managers at all levels in both primary and secondary schools have expanded to incorporate a plethora of new responsibilities and associated pressures.

A great deal of time and money has been invested in training heads, deputies and more recently middle managers in a range of management tools and techniques. Many of these have focused on improving the effectiveness of the organisation and on getting the job done with the greatest efficiency.

Much has been written on the subject of school management. Schools have become immersed in management initiatives and jargon. Teachers have had to bear the brunt of the "road to Damascus" management experiences of senior managers returning "all fired up" from management courses led by would-be management gurus. In many schools, however, organisational structures remain stubbornly hierarchical and inflexible, whilst approaches to management appear increasingly archaic.

Despite the pre-occupation with "management", many schools record increased workloads for teachers, the lowering of morale of many more and a general sense of innovation fatigue at all levels in schools. The Government's White Paper **"Excellence in Schools"** (DfEE; July, 1997) identified new priorities and challenges for the education system. In its wake, it promises more change for schools, with additional pressures and expectations on teachers and managers.

It is time to reassess management approaches in Education. Education is about leadership as well as management. For those who have spent a career in teaching it will be plain to see that "management by the stick" approaches that invest little trust in the professional judgement of teachers and ultimately disempower them, have little to offer schools. In the long run stick management stultifies creativity and innovation. It breeds fear and mistrust. It may work to alter behaviours in the short term, but over time it demotivates and succeeds only in encouraging people to avoid taking risks and making mistakes. In the context of our schools, the "effectiveness" experiment has simply encouraged teachers and managers to become ever more creative at finding ways to avoid the "stick."

This book aims to play a part in restoring the *human dimension* to the debate about what makes schools effective and about what makes them improve. It is less about management than *managing*; less about managing than *leading*. What successive governments have failed to realise is that the success of our schools depends on the well being of the people who work in them, both pupils and teachers. To lead and manage people effectively requires more than power and pressure. It requires a range of personal qualities and interpersonal skills. The effective deployment of these qualities and skills in a genuinely supportive and congruent way generates an ethos and culture that fosters learning. It can promote the intrinsic motivation in people at all levels in a school which is the only sure way of securing continuous improvement.

This book provides advice to existing and aspiring school leaders and managers - heads, deputies, heads of faculty / department, heads of year, heads of house, subject leaders and co-ordinators on how they can develop greater self-knowledge, understanding and skill in leading and managing themselves and others. This, hopefully, leads to interactions with colleagues that are positive, constructive and achieve shared goals.

Part One will focus on the development of a range of skills to help the individual manager to develop the personal skills and resources to manage and lead themselves effectively. To manage and lead others effectively it is important to manage and lead yourself. *Section One* will focus on the importance of outcome thinking and creative goal setting for success. *Section Two* introduces a range of practical strategies for effectively managing time and priorities. *Section Three* focuses on the importance of *state of mind* and the *beliefs* which underpin our behaviours to increase our personal effectiveness as managers. It introduces some techniques to effectively manage *resource states* and to explore relationships between a person's beliefs and his/her performance.

Part Two introduces a range of techniques that improve the quality of interpersonal encounters. *Section Four* focuses on the importance of *rapport* and *congruence* in dealing with people. *Section Five* introduces a model for recognising and responding to the language patterns of other people. Finally, *Section Six* introduces a range of processes for resolving differences between people in a sensitive and constructive manner.

Overall, the book is designed to make a contribution to the debate about what schools are for and to help managers in schools operate more effectively. It seeks to reassert the vital importance of quality relationships in the educational process. The ability to communicate effectively with oneself and with others is the key to successful learning in schools.

Setting Personal Goals for Success

> *In this section you will learn:*
>
> ☞ *About the importance of personal goal setting in motivating you towards successful achievement of your aims.*
>
> ☞ *How to develop well formed goals and how to take the necessary steps to implement those goals.*

1.   The Importance of Setting Personal Goals

"Would you tell me please which way I ought to go from here?"
"That depends a good deal on where you want to get to," said the cat.
"I don't much care where," said Alice.
"Then it doesn't matter which way you go," said the cat.

Alice in Wonderland, *Lewis Carroll*

It is the current trend for schools to review their aims and values, to envision the future and to establish long and short term goals and targets for development. Such processes are intended to generate a shared sense of purpose and to give direction to the work of the school, as it seeks to improve standards of achievement for its pupils.

In order to meet these challenges effectively, managers must be clear about their own personal contribution to the achievement of school goals and targets. Setting goals for success at an individual level can be an effective way of ensuring the necessary levels of motivation and commitment to guarantee success. Personal goal setting helps clarify priorities. It enables managers to distinguish more effectively between the urgent and the important and between the important and the trivial. It ensures that sufficient energy is focused on what really makes a difference to performance and diverts attention away from activities which exhaust the time and energy of a school manager to little real effect.

2.   The Psychology of Goal Setting

Personal goal setting generates energy and motivation because of the way we think as humans. Most people seek order in their lives. If we have a change or an upheaval such as moving house, changing a job, or even a death in the family, our natural instinct is to try to get back to a more settled and orderly situation.

When we set goals we deliberately throw our system out of order. We create a disjuncture between where we are right now, our *present state,* and where we want to be, our goal destination or *vision.* Humans are very inventive at finding ways of restoring order and so we begin to find the energy, motivation and creativity to get back to a more orderly environment. This is the essence of Gestalt theory. This gap between vision and present state is known as *cognitive dissonance*.

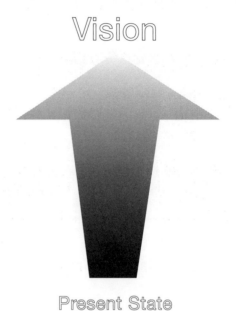

If our vision is vague and distant, we will find excuses for doing nothing to achieve it.

If our vision of the future is compelling enough we will move heaven and earth to move towards it.

In this unsettling gap between our vision of how things might be and our present state, we can select either route to restore order to our system, as the diagram above, devised by Chris Lindup, shows.

When our goal is clear, strong and vivid, we find ways of moving towards its achievement.

When it is vague and woolly - a wish rather than a passionate want - then it is unlikely to provide sufficient motivation to persuade us to take that important first step. We are more likely to consider all the pitfalls and talk ourselves out of the goal. We return to the safety of our current reality.

Most people are not short of goals. What they often lack are the reasons why they want to achieve those goals.

We tend to move towards the things which we find most appealing. It follows, therefore, that we must be very certain and specific about what it is we want to have, to do or to be - and the reasons why we want them - in order to generate the necessary motivation and energy to take action. It is important to create a strong and compelling enough image of what things will be like when the goal is achieved - to *see* the outcome, to *hear* it and to *experience* the feelings associated with its achievement, if we are to generate the necessary motivation and energy to move us towards it.

Much development work in schools is hindered by a premature concern about the *how*. Time and resources are the most common obstacles to development in the minds of many teachers. However, if you dwell too much on the obstacles in the way of achieving the goal, you are likely to talk yourself out of it and instead retain the *status quo*. As a result, you may become frustrated and disillusioned.

In contrast, by focusing strongly on the end result and initially ignoring the *how*, you are more likely to find the necessary energy and creativity to move towards the goal.

The brain provides us with the way to achieve the goal. The means to achieve it may be all around us. We may simply have not yet seen it. This is because a part of the brain called the *Reticular Activating System* acts as a filter and allows us to deal only with information which is important to us at any particular time.

When we set a goal, we invite our *Reticular Activating System* to give weight to information which will assist us in the achievement of our goal. For example, you may have at some time decided to buy a new car, perhaps a nice little red sports car. Now, there are thousands of red sports cars on the road. Many of these pass you every day and you do not notice them. However, when you set the goal, notice what happens. You see red sports cars everywhere. You notice special offers in the newspapers or on television. This is your *Reticular Activating System* at work. Set the goal and your brain will get very creative at finding the *how*!

3.   The Slaughterhouse Studio - A Case Study

> One night in a pub after an open evening, some teachers, including the head of drama, were lamenting the inadequacy of drama facilities at their secondary school in Bristol. The discussion turned to an old derelict building on the school site, used as a bicycle shed. It was the one remaining building from the old abattoir which had once stood on the school site.
>
> "Wouldn't it be great if we could do up the shed and turn it into a drama studio?" said one of the teachers. "We could fix up the roof, clear the old desks out and paint the inside black."
>
> "We could put down a nice wooden floor," added another teacher. "We could open it up for the community..." And so the discussion went on. The excitement was infectious. Bit-by-bit the vision of what became known as the "Slaughterhouse Studio" took shape.
>
> Within a year, plans had been drawn up. Someone knew an architect. Funding, both direct and indirect, was generated from the PTA and the school's budget. Someone had a contact with a local business who might be prepared to put in some money. A parent was a builder who was prepared to put in some work inexpensively.
>
> The project took on a life of its own and within a year the "Slaughterhouse Studio" was launched as an exciting new resource for the school and the local community.

4.   Personal Goal Setting in Action

The essence of personal goal setting is beginning with the end in mind. You need to become *end result oriented*. It is like standing at the top of the staircase looking down at what has been achieved rather than waiting at the bottom looking up at all those steps to be climbed. Personal goal setting is about *outcome thinking* - as opposed to *the problem thinking* which is so pervasive in our schools. All too often we concentrate on what is

---

wrong. Outcome thinking focuses our attention on what we want. It moves us forward towards the results we want, rather than simply away from what we want to avoid. Successful athletes such as Linford Christie and Sally Gunnell have employed creative personal goal setting and outcome thinking to improve their performances.

Personal goal setting does not have to be on the grand scale. We may all have significant longer term goals, but it is possible and even desirable to goal set on a daily or weekly basis. Most people already goal set without knowing it. On a daily basis they create images of what it will be like when a particular task is completed, or what the end result will be of a particular meeting, or even what they will do when they get home from work. These images generate motivation and energy to meet the challenges of working life.

Many teachers goal set to the end of school on Friday. Five minutes after the end of the school day they feel drained and exhausted. It is important to goal set up to and through the end of the school week. You need to goal set for Friday night and the weekend. Goal setting releases energy. When the goal is achieved the energy dissipates. The message is *goal set up to and through an event.*

5   Levels of Personal Goals

We can set *having goals* - generally to do with acquiring some new possession like a car or house.

We can set *doing goals* - typically about learning new skills or completing a task by a specified date.

We can also have *being goals* - largely to do with developing personal qualities such as confidence, calmness, etc.

There is no limit to the number of personal goals you can set. Goal setting helps generate the energy and enthusiasm to take the pain out of the most unpleasant tasks! However, it is important to remember that the setting of significant goals - particularly those related to the development of personal qualities - should be preceded by a careful analysis of what you value and feel to be of greatest importance to them in your life. Life-changing goals have significant knock-on effects for others and should be set only after careful consideration of all the possible consequences.

Ask yourself:

What will this goal achieve for me?

What could be the knock-on effects for myself and others of my setting and achieving this goal?

6. Guidelines for Personal Goal Setting

- Be clear and specific about what you want to have, to do or to be.

- Create a vivid image using pictures, sounds and especially feelings of what it will be like for you when the goal is achieved. (The more vivid the image, the stronger the emotional content and consequently the more compelling the goal.)

- See the end result in the present tense. Use emotive and evocative words. ("It feels really great to..."; "I really enjoy the feeling of...").

- Write down the goal. Once again, use the present tense to describe the goal having been achieved. Keep it where you can have regular sight of it. Recite the goal statement and recreate the imagery of its successful completion four or five times each day.

- Do not worry about the "how". Focus on the *end result*.

- Allow your unconscious mind to embed the goal and to generate the energy and creativity to find ways of moving you towards the goal.

7. Getting the Balance Right Between Personal and Work Goals

It is important to set work goals and personal goals to promote personal growth and development. It is also important that these goals are in balance and that no goal or set of goals consistently receive priority over others. Your goals should fit together in harmony. Work goals can conflict with non-work commitments. If we always give priority to our work goals then we may end up neglecting family and friends. The consequences of this might in turn rebound on our performance at work and detrimentally influence our prospects of achieving work goals. It is important, in setting goals, to consider the full spectrum of our lives. We should consider setting goals in relation to such areas as:

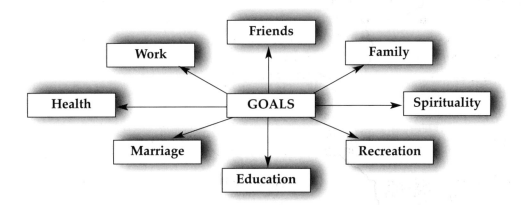

Managing our lives to ensure that we devote sufficient time and energy to achieving what we want to have, do or be in a totally congruent way requires careful planning. However, it will pay dividends in terms of happiness and the sense of personal satisfaction that comes from goal achievement.

Ask yourself:

> In which areas of my life do I regularly set goals?
>
> In which areas of my life do I never set goals?
>
> How do I decide on my priorities for goal setting?

8.   Clarifying your Personal Goals

Take some time to consider what is important to you at this moment in time in some or all of the areas of your life listed above. Write down on a table (see below) the five most important goals in each of your working and personal life. Remember a goal is the "end point" of a development, so write your goals with the sights, sounds and feelings of success in mind. Remember to distinguish between *having, doing* and *being* goals. Distinguish also between *long term, medium term* and *short term* goals.

Personal Goals	Work Goals

9.   Ensuring you have a Well Formed Goal

You may already be familiar with the **SMART** acronym in relation to goals. Goals should be:

Specific

Measurable

Achievable

Realistic

Time Constrained

Improving Personal Effectiveness for Managers in Schools

However, to ensure that you have chosen the right goals for yourself, and that those goals are clear and specific enough to generate the necessary motivation and energy to lead to their achievement, you need to put each goal through the following simple tests of *well-formedness*.

8.1   Ask yourself, "Is My Goal..."

Positive or Negative?

Definitely or Maybe?

Specific or General?

Evidence-Based or Wishful Thinking?

Mine or Someone Else's?

Positive or Negative?

Is the goal expressed in the positive? It is better to express goals in a positive rather than a negative way. Remember, we need to generate imagery of a compelling end result if we are to move towards our goals effectively. If we set a negative goal our brain processes imagery that is negative rather than positive. Make your goals those of aspiration rather than desperation. If your goal is phrased in the negative, ask yourself the question:

What would I rather have, do or be?

For example: "I want to stop worrying about my school work." (*Negative*)

"I want to feel confident and relaxed about my school work." (*Positive*)

Definitely or Maybe?

It is important to ask the questions:

Do I really want to set this goal?

What or who else might be affected by my setting or achieving this goal?

It is important do a personal ecology check. Goals are not set in isolation. Sometimes work or personal goals have consequences for our own lifestyle, or for that of others, that we may not be aware of at the outset. (See page 13) We might find these consequences unacceptable.

Many middle managers in schools set themselves the goal of achieving a senior management position without fully considering what effect this might have on their relationships with fellow colleagues or with their families. Remember to explore the implications of a particular goal before committing yourself to it.

Ask yourself:

> **If I could have this right now would I take it?**

If you answer yourself with a definite *Yes* then proceed. If you feel some doubts or reservations surface then take time to explore those doubts. It may well be that you are in danger of setting an inappropriate goal. Only when you are satisfied that the end result is what you really want and that you can deal with the consequences should you commit yourself to a goal.

Specific or General?

Is the goal specific enough? It is important to distinguish between vague wishes and real wants. We all have aspirations and dreams which in an ideal world we might have some hope of achieving. A goal is much stronger than this. It must be very clear and specific. For example, a work goal of raising standards of achievement in your subject area would fail the "specific" criterion. However, the goal of achieving a pass rate of 60% at grades A*- C in GCSE with a particular year group is clearly specific and measurable.

Ask yourself:

> **"Who, what, where, when, how specifically?"**

Evidence-Based or Wishful Thinking?

How will you know you have succeeded in your goal? What evidence will you be able to see, hear and feel which will let you know you have achieved it? What ongoing feedback will let you know that you are making progress towards your goal?

Tangible evidence such as examination results or an improvement in attendance statistics will form an important part of this criterion. But much more significant in terms of personal goals are the sights, sounds and feelings which accompany the achievement of the goal. It is this sensory evidence, and the expectation of experiencing it, which is the most powerful generator of energy and motivation to achieve the goal.

Many secondary teachers will recognise the feelings they have in late August when viewing the school's examination results. In particular, they will recall their sensations of relief, elation and satisfaction when their department's examination results are good. It is those sensations - rather than the results themselves - which underpin our work goals.

Ask yourself:

> **Is it possible to measure the difference between my present state and the achievement of the goal?**

> **What will it look, sound and feel like when I have achieved my goal?**

Mine or Someone Else's

What will you do yourself to achieve the goal? It is no use setting a personal goal if its successful achievement depends on the actions of others. You must take responsibility for achieving your own goals. Of course, you may have to work with and through other people, some of whom may not necessarily see eye-to-eye with you. Therefore, you need to plan for all eventualities. Most importantly, you must plan the first step which you personally will take on the road to the achievement of your goal.

Ask yourself:

What will be my first step to achieve my goal?

Whose help can I enlist to achieve my goal?

Personal goal setting provides you with the sense of purpose and direction which can so easily be submerged under the weight of demands made upon school managers. It can help maintain the energy levels and provide a vehicle for the proper assessment of your progress and achievements, that are so essential for continued motivation and enjoyment of your work.

In the next section, we will explore a range of strategies for ensuring that your goals are clearly prioritised and that you really are focusing on the activities which will make the greatest difference to your performance as a school manager and provide you with the highest levels of success.

Improving Personal Effectiveness for Managers in Schools

Section Two

Effective Time Management

> **In this section you will learn:**
>
> ☛ **The importance of effective goal and task prioritisation and be introduced to a number of techniques for establishing and sticking to priorities.**
>
> ☛ **About the evils of procrastination and how to motivate yourself to get even the biggest or most unpleasant jobs done.**
>
> ☛ **How to deal effectively with the many demands which people place on you and how to empower others to fulfil their responsibilities effectively.**

1.   Time Management equals Life Management

Things which matter most must never be at the mercy of things that matter least.

Goethe

There never seems to be enough hours in the day for the manager in a school. Much traditional management theory applies largely to the world of industry and commerce where the manager's job is mainly to manage. In a school, of course, most managers also carry teaching loads. In a secondary school, a typical head of department or year head will carry fairly close to a full teaching load. It is not unusual for deputy heads to have over a fifty per cent teaching commitment. Many headteachers are either timetabled for some teaching or provide cover for absent colleagues.

In primary schools, the situation is worse. Subject co-ordinators and deputy heads normally carry a full teaching commitment, whilst many heads have quite significant calls on their time in the classroom.

In recent years the situation has been exacerbated by the development of Local Management of Schools leading to increased responsibilities for school managers.

Bearing the load of such multi-tasked responsibilities renders the application of much management theory somewhat problematic. However, it is precisely because the school manager's time is at a premium, that effective time management is a crucial component of effective management overall.

The effective management of time is a key element in the ability of school managers to:

- ■ **manage all their tasks**
- ■ **respond proactively to the needs of colleagues, governors and parents**
- ■ **ensure the school meets the learning needs of its pupils**
- ■ (and last but not least) **to retain a life outside school!**

This juggling act requires great skill and begins with the *setting and prioritising of goals.* Whatever else you do as a manager, the ability to separate the important from the non-important - and also the important from the urgent - will pay rich dividends.

The key to effective time and life management lies in channelling your energies into what you determine to be of greatest importance and what will give you the most satisfying outcomes at any particular time. It is about focusing on becoming *effective* rather than simply seeking to be *efficient*. It is about working in a more focused way rather than simply pouring more of your time and energy, both at home and work, into a seemingly bottomless pit of demands.

1.1 Factors which Create Time Management Problems for the School Manager

Managers in schools, at whatever level, can themselves create unnecessary psychological pressures by the way in which they approach their various roles and responsibilities.

Key factors which have a detrimental effect on performance include:

1. A lack of clarity about personal and work aims, values and goals, and a failure to prioritise effectively by ascribing relative values to goals and tasks.

2. Inadequate motivational strategies which lead to procrastination and time wasting in relation to large or unpleasant tasks and flitting from one insignificant task to another.

3. A lack of skill in managing the many different people who make demands on a manager's time.

In the following sequence we shall explore each of the factors in turn and suggest some practical strategies for addressing each one to enhance the management of time and personal effectiveness. Firstly, we will look at ways of prioritising goals, targets and tasks more effectively. Then we will consider some practical strategies for improving motivation and overcoming the problem of procrastination. The final part of the sequence demonstrates some ways of dealing effectively, yet sensitively, with the many demands which colleagues can place on you.

1.2 Getting your Priorities Right

In *Section One* we learned how setting personal and work goals generates a clear sense of purpose and direction. Making choices about what is important and what is not - and how best to achieve pre-determined goals and targets - are the starting points on the road to the effective management of time.

However, it is not enough to establish goals and targets. Unless you are able to differentiate in terms of priority between what needs to be done, it is easy fall in to the "Busyness Trap". Many school managers declare how hard they work and how busy they are. Yet few may be able to point at the end of any given week to real achievements and a sense of personal satisfaction in a job well done.

Prioritising goals and targets is crucial if the most important tasks are to receive the most appropriate time and energy. The following technique for *prioritising* is one of many which can enhance personal effectiveness.

Five Step Method for Prioritising Goals

1. Identify five personal and work goals from the list you drew up in Section One. (See below.)

2. Take each goal in turn and ask yourself the question, "What will this goal get me?" Reflect for a moment on what you will be *seeing, hearing* and *feeling* when this goal is achieved.

3. Write the outcomes of your reflections in bullet point form in column 2.

4. When you have completed this process for each of the five goals, compare your responses between goals 1 and 2, then between goals 1 and 3, then 1 and 4, 1 and 5, 2 and 3, etc. Remember you are comparing the *sensory based evidence*. In each case make a definite and positive choice between the relative merits of achieving the two goals.

5. Put a tick in the appropriate box to record your preference in each case (see page 22). When you have completed the paired comparisons and recorded the results, add up the scores for each goal. The results will provide you with a priority order which has been generated by reference to the goal outcomes.

Establishing Sensory Evidence of Goal Achievement

	Personal or Work Goal	What will the achievement of this goal get me?
1	To improve my department's GCSE results by a least 10% next year.	• Pleasure at seeing those improved grades when they first arrive in August (visual). • Being able to say to myself and other members of my department "Well done!" Hearing others saying, "Well done!" (auditory). • Feelings of personal and professional satisfaction - a sense of pride and accomplishment (kinaesthetic).
2		
3		
4		
5		

Paired Comparison of Goal Outcomes

Choose between:	Goal 1	Goal 2	Goal 3	Goal 4	Goal 5
1 and 2	✓				
1 and 3			✓		
1 and 4	✓				
1 and 5	✓				
2 and 3			✓		
2 and 4				✓	
2 and 5		✓			
3 and 4			✓		
3 and 5			✓		
4 and 5				✓	
Total Preferences	3	1	4	2	
Rank Order	2	4	1	3	5

Once you have established your goal priorities in this way, remember to decide what needs to be done to achieve each goal and within what time scale. The order of priority may or may not be the single determining factor in the timelining of goals. However, it pays to be clear about *by when* you have to undertake key actions. You also need to ensure that you have logically sequenced those actions. This helps you to manage time more effectively in the long, medium and short term.

Sequencing tasks is vital:
1. **to avoid overload at any particular time;**
2. **to ensure a proper balance between actions to achieve your various work and personal goals.**

There will be any number of actions which might contribute towards the achievement of a particular goal. Remember to list only those actions which are likely to have the greatest impact. Apply what is known as the *Pareto Principle* or *80/20 rule* to help you.

Pareto was a 19th century Italian economist who first observed that 20% of Italy's population owned 80% of the wealth. When we apply this to the school context we might say, for example, that 80% of a teacher's time is often focused on 20% of the pupils, or that 80% of job satisfaction comes from 20% of the work. Although this is a rough and ready guide, you might usefully employ it to help identify the key steps towards the achievement of your goals. Ask yourself the question:

What action, or series of actions, will make the most impact on the achievement of my goal?

The table below provides a helpful planning format for goal setting. On it you can record your priorities, identify what has to be done to achieve them (the key steps) and schedule a time scale for each step.

Steps to Goal Achievement

	Goals in Priority Order	Key Steps towards Achievement	Time Scale for each Key Step
1			
2.			
3.			
4.			
5.			

1.3 Managing Time on a Day-to-Day Basis

Once you have clarified and prioritised long, medium and short term goals it is important to plan time on a monthly, weekly and daily basis with those goals in mind. Most managers are adept at making daily or weekly task lists. These can be helpful, but more often than not they represent a catalogue of what has not been done rather than what has been done. The results can be demoralising.

An effective task list has to be prioritised. It should relate to some extent to the achievement of longer term goals of both a work and a personal nature. Remember, taking your children swimming or visiting the dentist may well be as valid priorities as attending a meeting, especially if you have personal goals which relate to your family's well-being or your own health.

Where possible, each task should be given a deadline for completion. A simple method for prioritising a task list involves the use of an **ABC** coding:

A = Tasks of high importance and/or urgency.	These are tasks which have greatest priority and to which appropriate time must be dedicated.
B = Tasks of medium importance and/or urgency.	These are tasks which should be done but which may wait.
C = Tasks of less importance and/or urgency.	Such tasks might be done if time permits.

It is important to take care that the urgent does not always take precedent over the important. If you are to make inroads into your goals, you must give appropriate priority to those tasks that contribute to you achieving your goals. Keep your goals in view at all times as a reminder.

A further refinement in the prioritisation process is to list your *level A* tasks and prioritise those using a numerical system: *A1, A2, A3* and so on. This gives you a clear sense of the relative importance you should attach to the achievement of each task at any given time. It helps you make fine distinctions about how to use your time. It also helps in *defending* the time you set aside for tackling your priority task from the priorities of others. Being able to demonstrate a rationale for your planned use of time is a powerful weapon in rebuffing those who make unreasonable demands on your time.

Some additional tips

- Don't clutter your list with tasks which are part of your daily or weekly routines.
- Put a line through tasks as you complete them. Use a brightly coloured felt tip. It feels good to see the progress you are making!
- Re-prioritise the list when a task is completed or another added.
- If a C priority remains on the list at that level for more than a week ask yourself the question, *Do I really intend to do this?* If not, then consider removing it from the list!

2   Getting Motivated to begin Tasks

Procrastination is "the thief of time". We can all be very creative at finding ways of avoiding, or putting off, big or unpleasant tasks. Sometimes we put things off because we shy away from telling people things they might not want to hear. Sometimes the sheer size of a project is so daunting that we find ourselves doing other things instead. Alternatively, we simply find it difficult to motivate ourselves to start a task, perhaps because we do not see the value of it.

Procrastination is not always a negative trait. Sometimes putting something off has positive results if the resulting consultation and reflection lead to better outcomes. Mostly, however, procrastination causes additional stress and reduces effectiveness.

Most people know they are procrastinating - but they don't seem to be able to do anything about it. Instead they berate themselves about their shortcomings and thus further demotivate themselves.

For many people the root of the problem of procrastination lies in the various motivational strategies which they employ to persuade themselves to begin tasks. Connirae and Steve Andreas in their book **"Heart of the Mind"** (Real People Press, 1990) identify four common, ineffective motivational strategies:

1   The "Negative" motivator
2   The "Dictator" motivational strategy
3   The "Imagine Doing It" motivational strategy
4   The "Overwhelm" motivational strategy

2.1   The "Negative" Motivator

This is when someone motivates themselves by thinking of all the unpleasant things which will happen to them if they don't complete a particular task. They might think of the head's anger if they don't hand in their reports on time. They might baulk at the embarrassment of arriving unprepared to a departmental meeting. This type of motivational strategy can work well for some people. In some cases it is useful to think of what is worth avoiding. In some professions it is vital that all possible outcomes are considered. For example, airline pilots and air traffic controllers practise on simulators designed to throw up the worst possible scenarios. However, a manager in a school who motivates him or herself *only* by worrying about the implications of failure, is unlikely to be able to inspire and motivate others. Focusing on the negative consequences of, for example, an Ofsted inspection, can divert your attention from the positive aspects of your role as a manager and teacher.

Typically, from a sensory point of view, the *negative motivator strategy* looks like this:

Visual	Auditory	Physical
See disaster if you don't complete a task.	*Say "You should do it."*	*Feel bad.*

Strategies to overcome the Negative Motivator

- Take a few minutes to reflect on a task which you need to complete fairly urgently and which you are having difficulty motivating yourself to begin.

- Listen to your inner voice say enticingly how good it will b- complete. Notice what you will be saying to yourself ar saying to and about you. Note the tone of voice.

- Visualise, as vividly as possible, what you will see when t see it through your own eyes. Make the images big, bright,

- Describe to yourself what it will feel like when you have con successfully.

The new strategy should now look like this.

Auditory	Visual	Physical
It will be really great when this report is finished.	*See finished report.*	*Feel sense of satisfaction.*
DO THE TASK!		

It is important to recognise that the negative motivator works for some people to ensure their effectiveness. When adopting a new strategy, be careful that it does not undermine your effectiveness.

2.2 The "Dictator" Motivational Strategy

Some people order themselves into action in a stern and dictatorial tone of voice. Sometimes these voices can seem like the voices of parents or other authority figures from their past. The most frequently used words and phrases in this style are *have to* or *should* or *must*. This motivational strategy engenders feelings of disempowerment and lack of ownership of the task. The most common response to this approach is unwillingness to do the task, followed by procrastination. This motivational style suggests a lack of control over one's own life. In sensory terms the strategy works like this:

Visual	Auditory	Physical
See task	*Say (in stern voice) "You have to do it."*	*Feel bad*

Strategies to overcome the 'Dictator' motivational strategy

● Try changing **orders** to **invitations**.

● Use a softer, more friendly tone with yourself.

● Change phrases such as *I have to, I must* and *I should* into *It would be nice to* or *It will be really useful/valuable/interesting/rewarding, etc... to do this task.*

The new strategy will look like this:

Visual	Auditory	Physical
See task.	*Say (in soft, inviting tone) "It will be really rewarding to do this task."*	*Feel positive.*
DO THE TASK!		

2.3 The "Imagine Doing It" Motivational Strategy

Many people think of what it is like to do a task instead of seeing it completed. This is fine when you perceive what you are doing to be enjoyable and pleasurable. However, it has the opposite effect when you are focusing on what you perceive to be "chores" or unpleasant tasks. Motivating yourself to do something that isn't inherently fun to do is difficult and this motivational style can present a major obstacle to success in new and challenging areas. The "Imagine Doing It" strategy looks like this:

Visual	Auditory	Physical
See yourself doing enjoyable task.	*"This is fun."*	*Feel good.*
See yourself doing difficult or unpleasant task	*"This is awful."*	*Feel bad.*

Strategies to overcome the "Imagine Doing It" Strategy

● Visualise the task completed instead of seeing the task actually being done.

● Tell yourself what is important to you about having the task completed.

● Notice the feelings of having completed the task successfully.

Remember to use this new strategy only when actually doing the task appears unappealing and leads to procrastination.

The new strategy will look like this:

Visual	Auditory	Physical
See task completed.	*Tell yourself what is important about that.*	*Feel sense of satisfaction.*

DO THE TASK!

2.4 The "Overwhelm" Motivational Strategy

Many people put off starting a task by visualising it in its entirety. A major task, such as preparing the school development plan, can seem a massive, daunting block of work and feel overwhelming. When someone feels overwhelmed they usually feel incapable of beginning a task and tend to procrastinate. The overwhelm strategy can look like this:

Visual	Auditory	Physical
See large task.	*"How am I ever going to do this?"*	*Feel bad.*

Strategies to overcome the "Overwhelm" motivational strategy

The common approach to dealing with this strategy is to break the task down in to more manageable chunks. Remember the old joke; "How do you eat an elephant?" Answer: "One bite at a time."

To develop more positive feelings about the task you need to take the following steps:

● Create a visual image of the task.

● Move the image further and further away from you so that it becomes increasingly smaller and less threatening.

● Begin by seeing the whole task completed, then notice what series of smaller steps you took to get you to the completion of the task.

- Now you have a series of smaller more manageable tasks with which you might feel more comfortable.

- If any of the steps continue to appear too large and daunting, repeat the previous steps with each in turn until you feel happy about the way forward.

The new strategy will look like this:

Visual	Visual	Physical	Visual	Physical
See entire task.	*Move task way from you. See it become smaller.*	*Feel less daunted.*	*See smaller steps to achievement of the task.*	*Feel motivated to begin.*

DO THE TASK!

The key to learning a new motivational strategy or strategies is to begin by understanding your existing strategies and their strengths and weaknesses in different situations. It is also important to recognise that you will have been running your old strategy for a long time - and that in order for the new strategy to override the old, it needs to be rehearsed a number of times. Replay the new pattern several times in order to accommodate the strategy effectively. Practise the strategy on a number of different tasks over a period of time in order to install it in your subconscious. After a while you will not even have to try and will begin to use the new strategy automatically.

3   Handling People's Demands

The school manager faces time pressures on a number of fronts. First and foremost come the demands made by people both in and out of school. In school, pressure comes from pupils, parents, colleagues, governors, the Local Education Authority and more recently from Ofsted. Out of school, the pressures of family life, friendships, etc. demand attention. Teachers, by virtue of their commitment to the teaching profession, are often described as "people people" and building quality relationships is the key to a successful school. But the investment in relationships can consume time and be emotionally draining.

An "open door" policy may send strong messages about your accessibility as a school manager. It may also:
- divert you from completing the many important tasks which you may have prioritised.
- result in you assuming new problems and tasks which might be more effectively dealt with by someone else.

Openness, accessibility and a willingness to take on the problems of others can be a powerful virtue in a manager. It can also lead to the disempowerment of others and ultimately to the manager's energies and time becoming dissipated.

The ability to say no in certain circumstances may well be one of the most important lessons a manager can learn. Learning how to work effectively with people is essential to avoid overload and burn out. In this section you will learn some simple techniques for dealing with disruptions, for saying no gracefully, and for ensuring that problems are dealt with at the most appropriate level in the school's organisational structure.

3.1 Dealing with Disruptions

Planned work can be disrupted by people and events. Sometimes such disruptions are unavoidable and require action: cover for an absent colleague; urgent phone calls; distressed staff or pupils; fire alarms (false or otherwise!) all of which rightfully make calls on your time. There are, however, many other distractions over which you may be able to exercise some control in order to safeguard the time you may have allocated to dealing with priority tasks. Remember, allowing yourself to be distracted from a task may well be a form of procrastination. However, assuming you are determined to get on with a task, there are steps that you might take to ensure you are not disturbed:

- Find an appropriately quiet and isolated location for your work if that is possible in your school. (If you are working on a significant task which requires unbroken concentration there may be merit in working at home if at all possible.)
- Alert colleagues and secretarial staff of your whereabouts and your need for quality undisturbed time. Be ready to respond to urgent matters only. Say when you will be available to deal with routine or non-urgent matters.
- Ask office staff to take calls and unless urgent, give the caller a time when you will return the call.

Should you be disturbed then there are some ways in which you might deal with the distraction.

Using Body Language to Deter Interrupters

The first method is to use your body language to acknowledge the presence of the other person, but at the same time send a strong non-verbal message that you wish to get on with your work. The key is to retain your posture facing your work position, only turning your head to acknowledge the other person as in *Figure 1*. Continue to hold your pen or to keep your fingers on the keyboard. By retaining your closed working body position you are signalling that you do not wish to be disturbed. More often than not this will be enough to send the potential distracter on his or her way. You might well get the opposite response if you were to immediately drop your pen or turn way from the computer screen towards the other person with an open body position as in *Figure 2*. The non-verbal signal in this case is: *Come and join me - I could do with a break and a chat.*

Figure 1   *Figure 2*

Closed position discouraging interruption | *Open position encouraging interruption*

Using the "Five Stage Assertiveness Statement" to say "No" Gracefully

If a colleague is undeterred by your non verbal signals, then you may have to resort to a verbal response to the unwanted interruption. The following five stage statement allows you to make your position and feelings clear in a pleasant, yet assertive, manner in the face of all potential unwanted or unnecessary demands on your time.

The Five Stage Assertiveness Statement

Stage 1   Clearly and specifically identify the behaviour of the other person who is distracting you.

e.g.   "This is the third time in the last five minutes that you have interrupted me from writing this scheme of work."

Stage 2   Describe the tangible effects of the other person's behaviour.

e.g.   "When you interrupt me I lose my train of thought and that slows me down to such an extent that I am unlikely to get the scheme of work finished on time."

Stage 3   Describe your feelings about not being able to get on with your task.

e.g.   "The thought of not getting this task finished on time makes me feel really annoyed."

Stage 4   Ask them to leave you to get on with the task and suggest another meeting time.

e.g.   "I would really appreciate it if you would let me get on with this. I will see you after school."

Stage 5   Invite the other person to comment.

e.g.   "Is that OK with you. You don't mind do you?"

3.2   Avoiding Other People's Problems

One of the most common ways in which school managers prevent themselves from operating as effectively as they might do is by assuming the responsibilities and problems of other people. "Leave it with me" is the classic sucker line as a colleague presents you with a problem in a busy corridor, usually as you are on your way to a lesson. Before you know it, you have unwittingly increased your workload, relieved someone else of the responsibility for dealing with the problem, and assumed the responsibility yourself. As a result, your priorities are compromised and your carefully planned use of time goes out the window.

The "superhero syndrome" is a manager's worst enemy. It may be flattering to have people constantly coming to you with their problems knowing you will deal with them. However, in the end, taking on responsibilities which really should be dealt with by others, leads to the disempowerment of staff and ultimately to a loss of your own effectiveness.

It is an important principle in management that a problem should be addressed at the lowest organisational level appropriate for its resolution.

The deputy head, whose work is constantly interrupted by having pupils sent to her by a teacher unable to control a class, will appreciate the importance of this principle. Taking on other people's problems can lead to confused lines of communication and responsibility. It can also often mean that the problem does not actually get resolved by anyone!

To avoid the pitfalls of taking on other people's problems it is important to develop a clear strategy.

3.3 Locating Problems at the Right Level

Step 1   When approached by a colleague with a problem, ensure you both fully understand the nature and extent of the problem. Before ending the conversation, make sure that you are both in agreement about what should happen next to begin to address the problem.

Step 2   Ensure that both the level at which the problem should be dealt with and the most appropriate person within the school's management structure for dealing with are clearly identified.

Step 3   Make sure that before the person with the problem leaves, they understand clearly what their next step will be - whether that involves them in action themselves or making recommendations for action to you.

Step 4   Make a note of what you have agreed, ask for feedback within an agreed time scale on any actions taken, and remember to check yourself whether appropriate action has been taken.

If you practise this strategy, you will find that people will, in time, become more motivated to assume responsibilities for themselves, since you have clearly entrusted them with the next step. A further advantage you may notice is that people will think more carefully before approaching you with a problem, knowing that the discussion will almost certainly end with them assuming responsibility for the next step.

Being clear about your work and personal goals is an important first step in improving your own personal effectiveness. Being able to differentiate between these goals in terms of their relative importance is crucial in ensuring that your valuable time and energies are used to optimum effect. Once your are equipped with the ability to motivate yourself to get going on even the most daunting and unpleasant tasks, you will amaze yourself with what you are able to accomplish, even within the tightest of time constraints. Learning how to cope sensitively, yet assertively, with the many distractions and demands which others can place upon you as a school manager will help conserve vital time and emotional energy. This will ensure that you can operate as effectively as possible in juggling the multiple priorities which a manager in a school is required to deal with in the world of education today.

Section Three

Dealing with the Pressures of Leading and Managing in a School

> **In this section you will learn about:**
>
> ☞ **The value of adopting several perceptual positions from which you can observe and more fully understand an event.**
>
> ☞ **The importance of achieving and maintaining resourceful states in order to optimise your work. You will learn a simple and effective technique for anchoring positive resource states.**
>
> ☞ **How the beliefs you hold play a major role in either limiting your actions or empowering you to great things.**
>
> ☞ **Some simple techniques for changing limiting beliefs.**

He who controls others may be powerful, but he who has mastered himself is mightier still.

Lao-Tsu

The many demands and pressures of leading and managing in a school can sometimes feel overwhelming. They can occasionally leave one feeling powerless. Such feelings can generate stress and a subsequent loss of personal effectiveness. Dealing effectively with those pressures requires high levels of motivation and organisational ability. It also requires the personal resources to remain calm and focused under pressure. This section provides some simple strategies to enable the school manager to maintain optimum levels of personal effectiveness.

1.   Perceptual Positions

The concept of *perceptual positions* provides a useful starting point. Perceptual positions are simply different viewpoints from which one can observe any event or situation.

Having the ability to see an event from different positions is a very valuable skill for any leader and manager. It enables you to understand your position more clearly. It helps you understand the other person's point of view in any interpersonal situation. It also provides you with the flexibility to step outside a situation and ask the objective questions such as: What is going on here? What is the most useful thing I can say or do in this situation?

There are three main positions from which to view an event or situation:

First position The position from which you can view an event from your own point of view or through your own eyes.

Second position The position from which you can view an event through the eyes of a second person. (Putting yourself in the other person's shoes.)

Third position The position from which you can view an event as though you were a detached observer.

When applying this concept to a problem, it can be useful to create a separate geographical space for each position. You can then physically move between them to help differentiate between the sensory experiences when dealing with difficult problems or situations, as we shall see in *Section Six*. Moving in and out of the different perceptual positions, experiencing and re-experiencing an event or situation from different points of view, can help generate options for action which you might otherwise overlook.

An understanding of perceptual positions is helpful in mastering the techniques for creating and sustaining positive mental states which now follows.

2. Maintaining a Positive Mental Attitude

We all experience a range of emotions during our working week. Sometimes we feel positive about our life and work. At other times we might feel negative. We might be calm and confident in some situations. In others we might be tense and anxious. The degree to which we feel resourceful or unresourceful during the course of a day will, to a large extent, determine how effectively we perform and deal with the many situations which confront us as managers in school.

Make a list of the range of mental states you might experience in a typical day under the headings *Resourceful States* and *Unresourceful States*. For example:

Resourceful States	Unresourceful States
Calm	Anxious
Confident	Lethargic
Determined	Bored

Our state of mind very often determines how effectively we perform our many managerial duties. More importantly, it can affect our reactions to events and the nature and outcome of our dealings with other people.

A very valuable skill which we will learn about in the following pages is to have the ability:

- to recognise the signals or feedback which tell us what state we are either already in or likely to slip into;
- to change from an unresourceful mental state to a more positive and resourceful state.

Read the following instructions.

Become aware of your current state of mind. If you could describe it in one word what would that word be?

Now try to describe in detail the physical and emotional features of the state. You can notice how you are breathing. Is your breathing slow or fast, deep or shallow? Notice how your heart is beating. Become aware of any feelings you are experiencing and identify where in your body those feelings are located.

Notice, also, any sounds you are hearing, both internally and externally. Are the sounds near or distant, loud or quiet, soft or harsh in tone?

As you are experiencing this state you might have a series of visual images in your mind. If you do see a picture is it large or small, moving or still, coloured or black and white, framed or borderless?

Spend a few moments trying to classify the various elements of your current state.

The above process calibrates your current mental state. The ability to detect the signals - through your own biofeedback mechanisms - of an impending change from a resourceful to a less resourceful state gives you more choice in dealing with particular situations.

In a difficult meeting, or even a conflict situation involving a pupil, parent, governor or a member of staff, allowing yourself to be drawn into a negative or unresourceful mental state can lead to unsatisfactory outcomes which can contribute to feelings of stress. Have you ever noticed how a problem situation often seems worse when you are not feeling on top form yourself!

Different states of mind have different characteristics, and these characteristics are generated by your responses to different stimuli. Imagine how your state might change if you were suddenly confronted by a poisonous snake! You would experience fear, revealed by tense muscles, shallow breathing, pounding heart, etc.

Mental states develop in response to different stimuli and these responses are often generated at a very early age and deeply embedded in your subconscious, so that they become automatic and apparently beyond your control. This is why, when you are faced with a difficult situation such as giving a presentation to fellow colleagues or a parents' meeting, although you may want to remain calm, your automatic response may generate symptoms of stress. There are many occasions when we need a particular resource or state of mind to deal with a new or challenging situation. Achieving and maintaining a positive and resourceful mental attitude when it is most needed are the subjects of the next exercise.

2. Staying Cool under Pressure

Despite the fact that many of our responses to certain situations were learnt in the earliest years of our lives and are deeply embedded in our subconscious, they can in fact be unlearnt. A response to a given situation is simply to do with association - an automatic response to a given stimulus. For example, if you have been driving a car for some time, when you see a red light your automatic response is to put your foot on the brake. Your subconscious mind has simply associated *red light* with *foot on brake*.

If we can change the association we can change the response in most circumstances. If, for example, we can teach the subconscious mind to associate making a presentation to a large audience of parents or fellow teachers with feelings of confidence and calmness rather than fear and trepidation, we considerably improve the chances of enhancing our performance. That is the essence of what is known as resource anchoring.

Once you have mastered the technique of resource anchoring you can use it effectively to achieve and maintain resourceful mental states in order to maintain and enhance performance in a variety of areas of your work.

Achieving and Maintaining Positive and Resourceful States of Mind

Step 1	Be aware of your present state of mind using the feedback process described on page 35. (Are you tired, stressed, relaxed, confident...?) Decide if you are in an appropriately resourceful state for whatever you need to do. (**Motivated and focused** to write a report; **calm and confident** before a meeting.) If you are not in resourceful state, decide how you want to feel.
Step 2	Recall a time when you last felt as you would like to feel now. Remember as much detail of that occasion as you can. (When, where, who, sights, sounds, feelings). If you can't remember what it felt like then guess!
Step 3	Leave that memory and choose three **anchors**. Anchors are the triggers that associate an event with a series of memories, thoughts, sounds, feelings and mental images. (A favourite piece of music recalls fond memories, a child's comforter brings a sense of warmth and security.) You will need:

Visual anchor	Choose a brief remembered visual image which has some significance for you.
Auditory anchor	Choose a brief sound bite that you know well.
Physical anchor	Exert some slight pressure on a very specific part of your body (You could simply press your index finger and thumb together or gently squeeze a part of your upper leg with one or other hand. It is important to make this anchor as discrete as possible and to remember exactly where the pressure point is located. You may want to use it again!)

Improving Personal Effectiveness for Managers in Schools

Step 4   Go back again in time and relive your memory in as much detail as you can. Experience it as if you were actually there at the time.

Notice what you see. If you are in the picture, gently ease yourself out so you see the event through your own eyes.

Become aware of the sounds you hear. Are they loud, quiet, near or far? Notice the tone. Is it sharp or soft?

Notice your feelings. Where are they located - chest, abdomen, elsewhere?

Step 5   Give yourself time to fully re-experience the sensation - the sights, the sounds the feelings of having the resource you now want to recall.

When you are fully immersed in the memory, re-experiencing the resource at its optimum level (not before, not after) *simultaneously* apply the three anchors - **visual, auditory, physical**.

Now break the state. Look around the room, distract your attention before repeating **Step 4** again. You will need to repeat **Step 5** about four or five times, breaking state between each experience.

Step 6   If your recall of the experience has been vivid and full of emotion you should by now have made a psychological association between the three anchors and the experience of the mental state you want. You should be able to recall the experience of the resource you want by simply firing the anchors - just as with **red light = foot on brake!**

To test this, simply fire all three anchors simultaneously. Notice the response. You can begin to be aware of the sights, sounds and feelings associated with the resource you wish to experience. If not yet, then you need to repeat Step 5 until your recollection is even more vivid.

Step 7   Simply imagine the next time you will need to have the resource in question and simply fire the anchors and notice how your perceptions of the future event have changed.

With thanks to John Seymour for developing this material

You can use this process over and over again to generate a range of positive and resourceful mental states that improve your performance at school and help you to cope effectively with the many demands and pressures you manage.

3.   The Power of Beliefs

Our beliefs shape our actions. They either limit our scope for action or they empower us to develop positively in new directions.

In order to improve your effectiveness as a school manager and as a leader, it is important to develop greater self awareness and understanding of those areas of your life and work where limiting beliefs are holding you back and preventing you from realising your full potential. Alternatively, it is important to be aware of those areas of your life and work in which positive and empowering beliefs are playing a significant role in promoting your well being and development.

Chris Lindup's diagram (below) illustrates how it is possible to place limits on your potential by what you believe and expect of yourself and others.

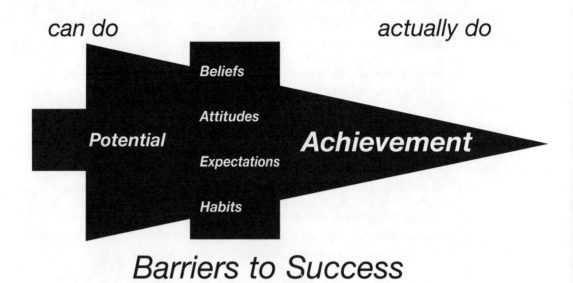

3.1 What are Beliefs?

Beliefs are no more than generalisations. Imagine a child who spends hours on the production of her first water colour painting which she duly gives to her mother as a present. Her mother is busy and preoccupied and her response, although well-intentioned, points to some shortcomings in the child's great opus. The child is disillusioned and generalises from the specific episode that she is not very good at drawing. A belief has potentially been embedded which the child may carry with her throughout life.

This is known as *imprinting*. Imprinting can occur as a result of traumatic experiences, constant repetition of behaviour, emotional intensity or conflict. For children, the words and actions of adults who are important to them, can be the source of many beliefs about themselves.

In such ways are beliefs, and indeed whole belief systems, generated. Beliefs become self fulfilling. If you believe you are not good at drawing, you will avoid art related activities. Henry Ford once said, "If you think you can do something or you think you can't you're probably right!"

Your beliefs affect your whole outlook on life. They affect your self image and self esteem in all aspects of your existence. They can lead to you feeling as if you are not in control of your life. They can lead you to become intolerant of others and to develop blind spots to the strengths and talents of yourself and others. They can also restrict your options in dealing with management problems. Once you lock on to a belief it is very easy to lock out other possibilities. It is no wonder that Christopher Columbus and Copernicus were scorned by their contemporaries. They were challenging some major belief systems at the time!

Look at the diagram below. What can you see? Perhaps a hat? a red indian? Can you see the fly?

If not, keep looking until it appears? Remember, by locking onto one way of looking at things, you could be locking out other possibilities!

A important skill in the development of personal effectiveness as a manager in a school is recognising limiting and empowering beliefs, as they impact on our own and others' lives. The development of this skill requires a great deal of focused reflection on the nature and origins of your beliefs and on their appropriateness. It is important to remember that some beliefs are very useful to us. To believe that one should always look left, right and left again before crossing the road is likely to be a good belief to hang on to. It may save your life one day! The value of many other beliefs, often generated in infancy, such as in the existence of the *bogeyman* may be limiting in the extreme.

Many beliefs, although useful earlier in life, may have become redundant and need revision.

3.2   Out of Date Beliefs

During the Second World War, the Japanese left garrisons on hundreds of tiny Pacific islands. With the advance of the American forces many of these islands were bypassed. When the war came to an end many Japanese soldiers remained marooned on a number of islands. Some were not aware that the war had come to an end and continued to fight the war, shooting at locals or passing fishermen. As time passed most were discovered and rehabilitated. The last one was found nearly thirty years after the war had ended. He had survived the elements and all the hardships that life on a remote island can bring. He still retained a stubborn loyalty to the Emperor and to his belief that he was fighting to protect his people. His beliefs, now long out of date, had sustained him through his struggles. His eventual return to civilisation had to be handled very carefully, for it required a gradual, but fundamental, shift in his belief systems.

This story of the Japanese soldier clearly demonstrates the power of beliefs and the importance of reviewing our beliefs periodically to discover if they are still useful to us or, whether with the passing of time and the advent of new situations, they have become limiting.

In developing our understanding of beliefs and their impact on our personal development we need to focus on four related concepts.

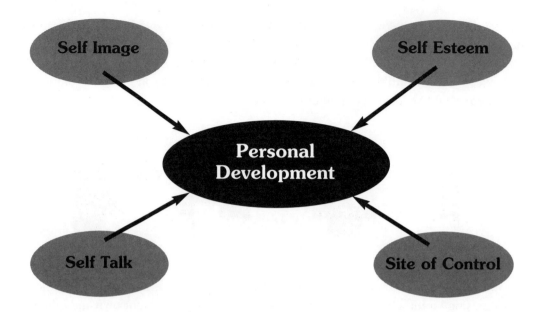

a. Self Image

We actually have many self images of ourselves: parent, teacher, manager, leader, golfer, driver, etc. Some of these may well be positive self images. For example, you may well see yourself as a good classroom teacher, but perhaps have misgivings about your ability to manage a team of people or even lead a school.

Our beliefs about our different self images can determine how we act in particular situations. Our self images are no more than beliefs about ourselves and like any belief, they limit our actions and make us what we are. In order to understand more fully what different self images you might have about yourself as a school manager, you need to ask some searching questions:

> Which aspects of my role as a school manager do I think I am good at?
>
> Which parts do I think I don't do particularly well?
>
> What do I think that I could never be able to do?
>
> How do I label myself? What labels do I allow others to give me ?

b. Self Esteem

Our self esteem is a measure of the value we give ourselves. It is affected by the accumulation of beliefs across a wide area which provides us with feedback - sometimes accurate, sometimes not - about the kind of person we are. Genuine self esteem starts on the inside. All too often, people take their self esteem from the house they own, the car they drive, the job they have.

People with high self esteem are outward looking, self confident and open to new ideas and responsibilities. In contrast, colleagues with low self esteem are frightened of change and try to maintain their own position by devaluing or running others down. They will very often feel as if they are not fully in control of their lives. They will often look to others for recognition and approval. Very often those with low self esteem will reject praise, even if they have done something well, simply because they feel they are not worthy. As a school manager, whose job is to manage, lead and motivate others, it is important to have a view of your own levels of self esteem. To lead others it is important that you are able to lead yourself! You might find it useful to consider the following reflective questions:

In which areas of my role as a school manager do I have a low opinion of myself?

How does that low opinion affect my performance and the way I work with other people?

To whom do I look for approval for my actions?

How do I try to put people down?

What in my job do I feel that I "have to" do?

How does the way I talk to myself help lower my opinion of myself?

c.   Self Talk

The way we talk to ourselves, our *self talk*, can reinforce limiting beliefs and lower self esteem and self image. On the other hand, positive self talk can enhance self esteem and self image. When you make a mistake how do you speak to yourself? Which of the following do you use?

There I go again, that's just like me or I'm no good at this sort of thing.
(Reinforcing limiting belief).

OR

That's not like me. I'll get it right next time.
(Reinforcing empowering belief).

The ability to *control* your self talk is an important protection against the gradual erosion of self esteem by the installation of negative or limiting beliefs. It is useful to reflect on the following questions:

What are some examples of negative self talk I use in school?

What are some examples of positive self talk I have used or have helped me?

What do I do when I hear negative, devaluing talk among my colleagues and pupils?

d.   Site of Control

This is the place where we believe control of our lives is located. For those people with high self esteem this is internal. For those who feel trapped and powerless victims of the "system" it is external. For teachers and managers working in schools, the perennial problem is retaining the belief that they have control of their working lives as dedicated professionals within a disempowering and often hostile environment. In order to have a clearer understanding of the extent to which you believe you are in control of your life it might be useful to ask the following questions:

> When do I blame others for the things that happen to me as a school manager?
>
> Where have I given up responsibility for an area of my managerial role completely?

3.3 Changing Unwanted Beliefs

Beliefs can be changed, although the more deeply embedded the belief the more difficult it is to change. What we call *core beliefs* which have been installed from a very early age - and which drive much of our behaviour - are very difficult to change. Indeed, it may not be wise to attempt to do so, since such beliefs may have a profound impact on our sense of identity. However, some beliefs as mentioned earlier, may no longer be appropriate. Some may simply be out of date and limiting your development into new areas.

It is useful to classify beliefs in levels. Beliefs at the level of *environment, behaviour* and *capability* may lend themselves more readily to change techniques. Those which relate to *values, identity* and indeed *spirituality* may require a more fundamental review.

3.4 The Different Levels at which Beliefs are Installed

Environmental
The outside things we react to such as our surroundings and other people. You might believe that you cannot work very well because of the state of your school buildings or the cramped state of your office.

Behaviour
What you actually do. You might have a belief that a certain way of doing a particular job is the only way to do it.

Capability
Your skills and abilities to handle a particular job (Understanding a new financial package or dealing effectively with conflict.)

Values
Beliefs which reflect what we feel to be of greatest value in life. (Whether we value consumer goods more than friendships or elitism in education rather than equality of opportunity.)

Identity
Deep seated beliefs about your very identity. The kind of person you are. (Shy, confident, principled.)

Spirituality
These are beliefs about the meaning of life and why we are here? They can give us our sense of life purpose.

As a manager in a school, dealing with people and their problems on a regular basis, it can be useful to be able to distinguish between the levels at which problems present themselves. It is all too easy to fall into the trap of treating the problems of others, and indeed of yourself, at an inappropriate level. Underperformance by a member of staff may have more to do with beliefs about their working environment, or a perceived lack of capability in a specific aspect of their work, than with a pernicious desire to undermine the management of the school! Taking time to find out the real motivation for people's actions is the hallmark of an effective leader and manager in a school.

3.5   A Simple Technique for Changing Unwanted or Limiting Beliefs

For changing limiting beliefs at the level of *behaviour, capability* or *environment*, a simple belief change process may be effective. To try this, choose a fairly low level belief connected with your working environment, or some capability you feel you do not yet have.

1.   Write down the limiting belief and say it out loud. Ask yourself where, when and from whom did this belief come?

2.   Confirm you really want to change this belief at this time and consider what the implications might be of changing it?

   If the answer to the first part of the question is a definite yes - proceed.

   If you begin to have some doubts, reservations or objections then explore them before proceeding.

3.   If you are certain that you would like to change the belief, continue by asking yourself what it would be more useful to believe.

   Word the new belief positively. Write it down and say it out loud.

   Notice, write down or recite any objections to the new belief. Continue until you have considered all objections.

4.   Imagine living with this new belief for a whole day. What problems might it cause you or others? Fine tune the new belief to remove the problems.

5.   Do a final check on the acceptability of the new belief. Ask yourself, "If I could have this new belief right now would I take it?" If you get a definite **yes** in response then go to it! If not, repeat steps 2-5 and explore again the doubts, reservations and objections.

With thanks to John Seymour for developing this material.

Robert Dilts' book **"Changing Belief Systems with NLP"** (Meta Publications, 1990) provides an in-depth look at the whole area of beliefs and belief systems.

The ability to keep a clear head and remain calm when others around you are flapping is a fundamental characteristic of the effective leader and manager. By remaining positive and resourceful under pressure you can improve your personal effectiveness considerably and thereby retain the ability to bring all your knowledge and experience to bear in dealing with even the most challenging situations. Developing a better understanding of the origins and power of beliefs to drive the behaviour of yourself and others can provide you with valuable new insights into the nature and causes of both your own personal doubts and fears and those of others. The ability to expose, and address limiting beliefs in yourself and others can be a powerful means for personal change and growth.

Improving your Communication Skills

> **In this section you will learn about:**
>
> ☛ **Some key principles in effective communication.**
>
> ☛ **Different approaches to interpersonal communication including the importance of rapport to the success of any interaction. You will be provided with some techniques for establishing and maintaining rapport to enhance communication.**
>
> ☛ **The concept of congruence as the key to trust in any relationship. You will also learn how to give and receive positive strokes to raise the self esteem and performance of others.**

To effectively communicate, we must realise that we are all different in the way we perceive the world and use this understanding as a guide to our communication with others.

Anthony Robbins

The quality of relationships between staff, pupils, parents and governors is a key indicator of the ethos of a school. Effective communication is the lubrication which promotes the smooth running of a school. It helps secure relationships of openness and trust which contribute to the learning of pupils. It is important to understand that in any interaction between people there are no truths - only perceptions. We all have our own "maps" of the world, each of which may or may not have some validity.

The essence of effective communication is trying to understand a person's map - to understand what makes them tick. It is important to acknowledge the feelings which underpin the other person's point of view in order to reach a mutually satisfactory outcome to any interaction. Disagreement - and often conflict - are the inevitable outcomes of the failure of two people to acknowledge the potential validity of each other's perceptions of a particular situation.

In this section you will learn some strategies for improving the quality of your interactions with colleagues. You will acquire greater flexibility in dealing with other people and so improve your performance as a manager. The individual with the greatest flexibility of thought and behaviour can (and generally will) have the greatest influence on the outcome of any interaction.

1.   Key Operating Principles in Effective Communication

Some key principles underpin this section. They are not truths which have to believed without question but they are guides for action. It is suggested that if you choose to act as if you believe them, then the quality of your communications and of your relationships with the people you work with as a manager in a school will improve significantly.

Principles of Effective Communication

1. You cannot avoid communicating. Whether you mean to or not, you are communicating, both verbally and non-verbally, all of the time. Sometimes you may be unaware of how you are communicating.

2. The meaning of your communication is the *response you get*, which may be different from the *one you expect*. If you are not getting the response you want perhaps you need to change the message and the way you transmit it.

3. We do not operate directly on the world. We create maps from our previous sensory experiences of life. However, just as a map is not the territory, so our perceptions of the world are simply perceptions.

4. There is a positive intention behind all human behaviour. Believing otherwise creates a negative intention where none exists.

1.2   Approaches to Interpersonal Communication

Stephen Covey in his book **"Seven Habits of Highly Effective People"** (Simon and Schuster, 1989) identified a number of possible models for the conduct of interactions between people. The discipline of *Transactional Analysis* mirrors these approaches in the shape of what is known as the *OK Corral*.

Win/Win (I'm OK. You're OK)	Lose/Win (I'm not OK. You're OK)
Win/Lose (I'm OK. You're not OK)	Lose/Lose (I'm not OK. You're not OK)

Win/Win (I'm OK. You're OK)

In this model both parties communicate effectively in order to achieve an outcome which pleases both. It is based on the belief that collaboration can produce mutually beneficial results: that the whole is greater than the sum of the parts. It often involves the parties moving from focusing on my way or your way to a third or better way. It relates to the *I'm OK. You're OK* analogy in Transactional Analysis.

Covey suggests that this model underpins what he calls *Principle Centred Leadership*. It helps build better relationships within an organisation, but it requires high courage and a high level of consideration for each other's views. It is a fundamental premise of this book that the *win/win* model of human interaction should underpin the leadership and management culture within all schools.

Win/Lose (I'm OK. You're not OK.)

This model is based on the view that there must inevitably be winners and losers. Such a belief may have relevance in sport, but when it is practised in the school it reflects a hierarchical and bureaucratic approach, rather than a collegiate approach. It leads to disempowerment and to feelings of resentment and demotivation. It is the equivalent to the notion of I'm OK. You're not OK - hardly a recipe for effective leadership in a school! Covey suggests that this model may require high courage but reflects a low level of consideration for the feelings and views of others.

Lose/Win (I'm not OK. You're OK.)

This approach implies that one party abdicates responsibility for the success of the organisation to others, often because they do not feel they have the capability to perform certain duties. In schools this is often exemplified by such comments as, "Let them do it-they're getting paid for it". It can also be a means by which colleagues justify their lack of success by pointing to the defects of the system, or in the case of schools, on perceived shortcomings of the senior management team. In the OK Corral this equates to *I'm not OK. You're OK.* Stephen Covey suggests that such a approach requires low courage and high consideration.

Lose/Lose (I'm not OK. You're not OK.)

This is all about reaching compromise, but one whose outcome satisfies neither party. It's a cop out and suggests low courage and low consideration. In a school situation this could mean that poor teacher performance or disciplinary problems are not addressed because neither party is prepared to deal with the issues assertively. In *OK Corral* terms this relates to *I'm not OK. You're not OK.*

Covey describes another possible approach to interpersonal transactions which is about winning at all costs. *I will get what I want and to hell with the consequences.* School management can be a very lonely business with this attitude!

Understanding the nature of a particular interaction, particularly if you are able to view it from first, second and third positions, can provide you with a context within which you can deploy the appropriate strategies to bring about a successful outcome to the interaction. Central to the success of any interpersonal communication is the quality of *rapport* and the degree of trust which can be engendered between the parties through the vehicle of *congruence*.

2.   The Magic of Rapport

Rapport is fundamental to the effectiveness of leadership and management in schools. It can be defined as a relationship between people which is characterised by harmony, understanding and mutual confidence. Our life experiences are unique to us. They shape our values, beliefs, habits and attitudes. They develop our different "maps" of the world. If you gain rapport with someone, they feel that you acknowledge, understand and value their opinions. You don't have to agree with them. Rapport is not simply about agreement. You can disagree with someone and still remain in rapport with them.

Rapport creates the conditions in which relationships that promote effective working are more likely to be created. The absence of rapport between people can create mistrust and leave people feeling undervalued. In the longer term it can lead to misunderstanding and conflict within a school. In contrast, when two people are in rapport, their energies can be more easily synchronised to reach higher levels of achievement. Rapport is a key element in the motivation of people in a school.

Exercise - the Power of Rapport

Find a partner who is willing to try this exercise with you. Choose someone whom you may not know particularly well. The exercise should only take ten minutes.

Find a quiet space and sit down square on to each other. Ask the other person to talk freely for a few minutes about something which they find particularly interesting (a recent holiday, a project they may be working on, a hobby.)

As they speak, listen very intently. Show obvious interest in what they are saying. You could feedback some key elements of what they are saying to emphasise how carefully you are listening. Nod appropriately in acknowledgement and understanding. Lean forward and maintain eye contact. Try to match your partner's body language. Do this for about one minute.

Then, very slowly and unobtrusively, begin to lose interest. Break off eye contact. Shift your body position so that you are beginning to turn slightly away. Don't acknowledge what they are saying. Do all of this very subtly and slowly. Notice the difference to your partner's conversation.

Stop after a while. Ask your partner for their comments on what happened when you began to show a lack of interest. How were they feeling? What were they hearing? What were they seeing?

Reverse roles. Choose an interest of your own to talk about. Your partner should act exactly as you did, at first very attentively and then gradually losing interest. Describe your feelings as your partner loses interest in what you are saying.

This exercise provides a practical demonstration of the power of rapport and of the consequences of the failure to achieve rapport in any interaction. Just as rapport between the teacher and the learner is crucial to the learning process, so rapport between head and staff - and between the staff themselves - is essential to the effective management of the school.

Knowing about the power of rapport is one thing. Taking the necessary steps to build rapport between people is another. Rapport is created not so much by what people say to each other, but by more subtle and often unconscious signals from what we call body language. While the words may carry the content of the message, the body language serves to transmit the nature of the relationship. If the words and body language convey conflicting messages, we tend to accept the non-verbal message as the more significant.

2.1   Achieving and Maintaining Rapport

Establishing rapport requires close attention to detail both in terms of the verbal and non-verbal communications. It requires the ability to mirror the other person's physiology in a number of different respects and to listen very attentively for specific patterns in the language of the other person in order to pace them. *Pacing* is the process by which you show that your are "paying attention" to the other person: that you are acknowledging and respecting their feelings and opinions. If the object of rapport is to influence the other person more effectively in order to lead them towards a *win/win* outcome to the discussion, then pacing is essential.

Pacing and *Leading* go hand in hand. It is very difficult to lead someone if you do not first pace them. Conversely, when you pace someone during the course of a conversation, you are much more likely to engage their interest and induce a more positive mental state.

Pacing involves:

- *Mirroring* the other person's shifting physiology as closely and as subtly as possible.

- *Active Listening* for clues in the other person's speech to find their preferred sensory channel - auditory, visual or kinaesthetic - and responding using appropriately matched language.

   Active Listening also enables you to match the voice tone of the other person and to demonstrate that you are acknowledging, understanding and respecting the views of the other person.

Mirroring

Mirroring involves the close matching of various aspects of a person's body language divided into the following areas:

1. **Body Position, Posture and Movement**
   Face the other person. Try to match as closely as possible their initial posture and orientation.
   If they are standing or sitting down follow suit.
   Be subtle in following movements.
   Respect their personal space. (Remember the concept of personal space varies from culture to culture.)

2. **Eye Contact**
   Match the level of eye contact which the other person gives you.
   Avoid staring. It can be off-putting.

3 **Hand, Arm, Feet and Leg Gestures**
   Match significant gestures indirectly. If a person crosses their legs you can mirror this by crossing your arms . This is called *cross-over matching*.

4. **Facial Expressions and Mannerisms**
   Facial expressions send powerful emotional messages. You can match them quite easily. Mismatched facial expressions are the most obvious inhibitors of rapport.
   Be careful with individual mannerisms. You can mirror any mannerisms though cross-over matching. If a person nods a lot, then you can mirror this by moving your fingers in a similar rhythm.

If you watch two lovers or friends engaged in conversation you will notice how closely they match each other's body language. It almost appears to be like a dance. They are not even aware that they are mirroring each other.

The challenge for those developing the skills of rapport is to be able to mirror all of the above features in an elegant and unobtrusive way. Crude mimicry of body position and individual mannerisms could actually offend the other person and inhibit the development of rapport.

Active Listening

Active listening is vital to the pacing process which is so important in the development of rapport. It involves three ingredients.

1. Listening for, and mirroring, sensory based language.

2. Listening in order to match voice pitch, tone, speed, volume, inflections and emphases.

3. Listening attentively to the content of the conversation to gain - and then demonstrate - understanding by feeding back key words and phrases.

a.   Mirroring Sensory Based Language

Our language can provide clues to what and how we think. It helps the listener pace more easily the inner experience that underpins what someone is saying. This is crucial in establishing rapport effectively. Imagine people leaving the cinema having watched the same movie. One declares, "The *scenery* and the *special effects* were spectacular." For the second, "The *soundtrack* and the *script* were brilliant." While for the third, "The story was very *moving*: a real *tearjerker*."

Each experiences the movie in very different ways. The first uses visual words, the second auditory and the third kinaesthetic to describe their experience of the movie. We all, of course, describe experiences in words, pictures and feelings. But we all have a preferred way of representing our experiences.

We also use specific words which indicate our *preferred representation system*. These words are called *predicates*. Listening carefully for predicates in the language of a person - and matching those predicates in conversation - are powerful ways of pacing and building rapport.

The table below lists some examples of *sensory based predicates* used in conversation.

Visual	Auditory	Kinaesthetic
I see what you mean.	*We're on the same wavelength.*	*This is a sticky situation.*
It appears that...	*In a manner of speaking.*	*Hold on a second.*
Show me.	*That rings a bell.*	*I can't put my finger on it.*
Let's have a close look at this.	*Sounds good to me.*	*Get a grip on yourself.*
Try to see things my way.	*What makes him/her tick.*	*This will only scratch the surface.*

Take five minutes to list as many examples of visual, auditory and kinaesthetic predicates, either single words or phrases, as you can.

Listening for predicates to identify a person's preferred representation system requires practice and skill. However, once you have determined it, you can try to enter that person's world by trying to match their language. For example:

"I'd like to *have a word* with you. I think we should *discuss* plans for the open evening and I would like to *talk you through* the arrangements so far."

"*Sounds good* to me. I *tell* you what. Let's *talk it* over after the senior management team meeting on Wednesday."

Read the following example then devise an appropriately paced responce for the other statements.

Example

Statement	*I don't **see** how this will work.*
Response	*OK, let's **look** at some alternatives.*

Surely you can see my point of view.

You haven't heard a word I've said.

How would you feel in my position?

I would like to toss some ideas around with you.

We don't seem to be hitting it off with each other.

I would like to examine this more closely.

I want you to tell me word for word what she said.

You don't care about hurting people's feelings.

b.   Voice Matching

Matching aspects of a person's voice can assist rapport. It requires close listening skills and keen sensory acuity. Features of voice to pay attention to include:

● the pace or speed at which a person is speaking

● where and when she/he pauses

● the volume at which she/he is speaking

● voice tone

● voice pitch (high or low)

● the phrasing of sentences

● any inflections and emphases on particular words or phrases

● favourite or regularly used words or phrases.

Practice

During your conversations over the next few days pay close attention to the various features mentioned above. Begin by becoming more aware of each feature in turn, as used by a range of people. Next, try to match one feature at a time of someone's voice.

When you feel confident enough, try matching two features, then three, four... until you feel skilled enough to begin to link your voice matching skills with your ability to pace sensory based language.

c.   Active Content Listening

Whilst establishing rapport through the matching of physiology, voice and language is crucial to the success of any interpersonal communication, an understanding of the content of the communication is essential to a successful outcome. It is also a prerequisite to the effective fulfilment of any future actions which arise from the conversation. Effective listening can be undermined in a number of different ways. For example, if the conversation takes place in an unsuitable environment there may be distractions and interruptions.

If the timing of the encounter is inappropriate, either party might well be preoccupied with other work issues and easily lose track of what is being said. When either party is anxious about the nature and outcome of the conversation they may feel the need to talk rather than listen. Individual insecurities can lead to one or other of the parties becoming engrossed in what they are going to say next, rather than listening to what the other person is saying. In order to create the optimum conditions for effective listening it is important to ensure that:

- The location is appropriate for the purpose. For example, a one-to-one conversation about personal issues should always take place in the quiet and privacy of an enclosed office.

- A sufficient amount of uninterrupted time should be allocated to facilitate the development of rapport and to avoid distractions.

- Seating arrangements should facilitate eye contact and active listening as well as putting people at their ease.

To listen effectively:

- Give your full attention to the speaker.

- Try to maintain good eye contact at all times.

- Show you are listening by nodding, smiling, giving signs of encouragement.

- Show interest and remember what is being said.

- Replay key words and phrases they use in order to acknowledge what they are saying.

- Allow periods of silence for the speaker to think what to say and to respond to your questions.

- Listen with an open mind. Remember we all have different "maps" and belief systems.

- Remember you are there to listen. Let the other person do the talking.

Conversely, do not:

- Show indifference, criticism or impatience through your body language or by what you say.

- Stare or look blankly as if you do not understand or are not listening.

- Look away from the speaker and so break rapport.

- Let your mind wander to other things.

- Interrupt the speaker.

- Fill in silences.

- Distract yourself by thinking about what you are going to say next.

- Make early judgements about the speaker or what they are saying.

- Notice only the spoken words and miss the impact of gestures.

3.   Congruence - the Key to Trust

We have all at some time listened to someone speak and have not felt convinced by what they have been saying - perhaps a politician on television, or a pupil protesting innocence. There may have been something about them which simply did not ring true. The words may have seemed convincing enough, but there was just something about the individuals concerned that led us to have reservations about them. There was something *incongruent* about them.

In contrast, we can all recall occasions when a person has inspired us by the force of their message. We believe and trust them implicitly. They appeared entirely *congruent*. *Congruence* is the key to trust when dealing with people.

The Latin origin of the word congruence suggests an agreement. A person can be said to be congruent when their behaviours are in harmony with their beliefs. When they conflict, and the person appears to act in contradiction of what they believe to be the truth, they are incongruent.

In a congruent communication, both the body language and the tone of voice support the verbal content.

An incongruent communication is one in which the words do not appear to match the body language and/or voice tone of the person. They send a mixed message. This can be either conscious (e.g. lying) or unconscious (e.g. doubt, uncertainty, inner conflict.)

The development of an enhanced awareness of congruence and incongruence in yourself and in others is particularly useful in one-to-one interactions where a better understanding of the other person's thinking can help unlock barriers to effective communication. When discussing plans for the future, it is very useful to have a feel as to whether or not a person is really committed to the agreed action. If their agreement to a new goal or target is incongruent, you are likely to get either conscious or unconscious sabotage of the action!

Similarly, it is important that you play your own part in ensuring that your part of the communication is congruent. Just as you may detect any hint of incongruence in the message of the person with whom you are communicating, so you should be aware that they may also detect signs of incongruence in your conversation.

One area where congruence is vitally important in developing rapport, trust and in building self esteem, is in the giving and receiving of strokes.

3.1   Giving and Receiving Strokes

As a school manager, one of your key roles is to ensure that the staff and pupils with whom you work feel valued and respected. It is important to give praise when it is due on a regular basis and also to identify areas which need development. The main instrument for giving recognition is the stroke. Giving - and receiving - strokes in a constructive and congruent manner involves a considerable degree of skill.

There are three main kinds of strokes.

- **Positive**
- **Negative**
- **Plastic**

3.2   Positive Strokes

However you give a positive stroke it will do some good. But it is much more effective if you do it well and with congruence.

The least effective stroke is a very general or globalised message. *You are doing a great job* or *You've all done very well* are pleasant statements to receive but they do not provide enough directed and precise information to be very highly valued. The stroke that is most appreciated is one that:

- is addressed to one specific person

- indicates the specific behaviour or situation which you appreciate

- indicates the tangible effect it has on you

- expresses your feelings about the other person.

For example:

Sally, I am really grateful to you for helping me with the costume changes during the school play last night. The changes were carried out so smoothly and efficiently that it made my job as director a lot less stressful and I really appreciated that.

Such a message is more likely to be valued than:

Thank you for all you've done.

It is important to emphasise that the body language should be totally congruent with the verbal message. To express appreciation of a specific action while gathering up your papers, looking at the clock, or gazing out of the window, takes away most of the effect!

Receiving Strokes

A person's ability to give and receive strokes is related closely to their level of self confidence and self esteem. People with low self esteem find it difficult to give strokes and often will simply not accept positive strokes. They may feel that they are not worthy of the praise or they think that the other person does not really mean it - or has an ulterior motive. People with high self esteem use strokes to reinforce their own self esteem. The skill of giving and of receiving strokes with precision and with congruence is a valuable one to learn, particularly within the school situation.

3.3 Negative Strokes

Negative strokes can be given inadvertently, often by means of a throwaway line. *You made a fool of yourself acting like that* or *Those shoes don't go with that dress.* are comments which by design or otherwise send a negative message. They result in unpleasant feelings for the recepient of these negative strokes. They send the message *I'm OK. You're not OK.* Take care that rapport is not undermined within your school by the persistent and insidious use of negative strokes and sarcasm.

3.4 Plastic Strokes

Worse still are strokes which are manipulative and incongruent. For example, *John, there is no one else who can do this job* or *If you take this one there could be a scale point at the end of the year.* A manager who persistently employs plastic or manipulative strokes as management tools will soon find that s/he commands little respect among colleagues. This eventually undermines the basis for effective leadership, motivation and teamwork that is needed to achieve the school's aims and goals.

By using the techniques described above systematically, and with elegance, you will gradually become adept at pacing and achieving rapport with all but the most difficult characters. The development of rapport skills, and an understanding of the importance of congruence when dealing with people, can bring improvements in your effectiveness in such areas as:

- *pacifying angry parents, colleagues and pupils*

- *addressing issues of teacher performance*

- *improving teacher and pupil motivation*

- *handling meetings*

- *dealing with difficult or sensitive situations*

As a result, the quality of relationships with colleagues, and within the school as a whole, will improve. This, in turn, will bring a significant improvement in your ability to lead staff more effectively towards the achievement of the long term aims and goals of the school.

It is important to recognise that naturally good communicators already exhibit these skills without realising it. However, breaking down these skills and practising their use consciously in a variety of different situations can improve personal effectiveness.

Initially, deploying the skills involved in building and maintaining rapport will seem unnatural and contrived. However, with practice, you will develop what is known as *unconscious competence* in their use, and add considerably to your toolbox of communication skills.

Section Five

Turning Language to Your Advantage

> **In this section you will learn:**
>
> ☞ **How to change the frame in which a person perceives an event in order to change the meaning and subsequent responses and behaviours.**
>
> ☞ **How to ask quality questions and to recognise a person's thinking patterns from the language they use.**

1. Reframing - Changing the Meaning of Language

There is nothing either good or bad, but thinking makes it so.
Shakespeare

The meaning of any experience or event in life depends to a large extent on the context or *frame* in which we place it. The *frame* may have a great deal to do with our past experience and our own particular *map* of the world. Whether a bottle is half full or half empty depends on your outlook. If you change the frame, you change the meaning of the event and generate different responses and behaviours.

Reframing is a useful skill which helps you see any event or experience from a different perspective, thereby become more creative in dealing with problems. It can help you represent your experience in a way which provides opportunities for new learning and development. The alternative is to bog yourself down in a *cul de sac* of negative thinking.

Reframing is not new. Many jokes, metaphors and fairy tales are based on an element of reframing. Good teachers use reframing regularly in order to encourage children in their learning. At its simplest, reframing simply involves changing a negative statement into a positive one by changing the frame of reference used to perceive the event. For example:

Negative Statement *My head of department is always on my back.*

Response *She obviously wants to prepare you for promotion.*

There are two main types of reframes:

- *Context Reframes*

- *Content Reframes*

2   Context Reframing

Context reframing is based on the assumption that most behaviours have a use or value in some situation or other. It involves taking an unpleasant experience or behaviour and showing it to have value or usefulness in another context. The ugly duckling suffered shame and ignominy among his fellow ducklings before taking his rightful place among the swans. If the headteacher were to turn up to a meeting of the board of governors in torn jeans and tee shirt, it might raise a few eyebrows. And yet, when gardening or decorating at home or on holiday, such garb is most appropriate. More seriously for schools, 35% of pupils achieving five A*- C grades at GCSE might appear low in a "leafy suburb" school, but represent an excellent achievement in a school where a high proportion of the pupils are disadvantaged. When using context reframing, the essential question to ask is:

Where else might this behaviour be useful or valuable to me?

The key is to try to find a more appropriate context in which the behaviour might be useful and then use that information to reappraise the initial behaviour.

Context reframe the following statements:

> *He's too much of a daydreamer, full of half baked ideas.*
>
> *I'm too indecisive when the head puts me on the spot.*
>
> *She's too flippant in senior management meetings.*
>
> *I'm too soft on her.*

3   Content Reframing

Content reframing involves taking a behaviour or an experience and simply changing its meaning. For example, you might say that a member of staff is always putting up obstacles to developments at faculty meetings. After content reframing, you might say that she has a good analytical brain and can spot potential pitfalls better than many other members of staff. The parent who is always complaining to the school may be seen as a nuisance or as a valuable sounding board for parental views on a range of school issues. The story is told of the famous general who was reported to have reframed his army's retreat by saying: "We're not retreating. We are advancing in another direction."

The worlds of politics and economics thrive on content reframing. The government can see high interest rates as good for inflation and economic stability. The business community sees only higher debt charges and threats to commerce and industry. At an individual level, content reframing involves taking statements which describe a person's behaviour and asking the questions:

What else could this mean?

What is the positive intention of this behaviour?

Apply those questions to the following examples.

I never get a word of thanks or praise from my head of department.
or
I panic when I have to stand up in front of the staff.

Some Practice...

> Think of something which did not go very well for you in the past year. Don't be surprised if you get a sudden rush of negative feelings associated with this experience! Consider whether this particular episode was part of a much wider set of experiences which included more successes than failures. As you consider it, begin to notice what you have learned from this experience and how you might handle a similar situation in the future.

You can home in on what you did wrong and continually replay the experience with all the associated negative feelings, or you can reframe the experience in a way which helps you grow and develop.

Remember there are many meanings to an experience. The meaning - or frame - you choose to emphasise will determine whether you turn the experience into something that works for you or against you. This is the essence and value of reframing. Reframing is a key element in the learning process and a useful tool for school managers in dealing with pupils, parents and fellow staff.

4   Sleight of Mouth Reframing Patterns

A popular model for reframing (taken from the discipline of Neuro-Linguistic Programming) is the *sleight of mouth* model. It provides the opportunity to consider a statement from a range of different viewpoints and offers a number of possible ways of reframing the statement to achieve a more positive outcome. This offers the possibility of releasing creativity within both individuals and teams of people.

An example of a problem statement common in schools is:

I can't do my job properly unless you give me more time and resources.

The following are examples of a range of responses which you might draw on to reframe the statement. You may need to try several before you get the response you want. Having such a toolbox of responses gives you greater flexibility when confronted with negative views.

We could talk about how you could make better use of the time and resources you already have. (**Identify a more positive outcome in relation to the problem.**)

Perhaps you need to change jobs. (**Explore the negative consequences of the problem.**)

Would it be useful if you undertook some training in time management? (**Set a further outcome to try to address their concerns.**)

It's a bit like the miracle of the loaves and fishes... (**Use a metaphor to depersonalise the problem.**)

You may be pressurised now but it will get easier as you get to grips with the job. (**Place the problem in a different time frame.**)

Budgets are tight everywhere.
or
Perhaps you're just feeling under pressure generally. (**Set the problem in a broader context.**)

How do you feel the job should be done properly?
or
What is important to you about doing your job properly? (**Explore their personal values in relation to the problem.**)

Perhaps you have too high expectations of yourself. (**Redefine the problem.**)

Are there wider problems which are preventing you from doing your job properly. (**"Chunk the problem up" to see if there are wider problems affecting their ability to do the job effectively.**)

Which particular part of your job are you having particular difficulty with? (**"Chunk the problem down" to more specific areas of their work.**)

Has there ever been a time when you achieved success when under pressure? (**Present them with a counter example to focus on prior achievements.**)

This shows that you set high standards for yourself. (**Focus on their positive intention in feeling that they need more time and resources.**)

Maybe you're worrying yourself unnecessarily by focusing on the whole of your job rather than its separate parts. (**Focus on how they are allowing themselves to worry about the problem.**)

You have probably used some or all of these different ways of reframing a problem in the past with varying results. In that respect they are not new. However, taken together, these *sleight of mouth* patterns provide a useful checklist. When addressing an issue, either individually or within a team, they provide new angles on a problem and unlock the creativity which promotes continuous improvement within your school.

5   Asking the Right Questions

Human language is like a cracked kettle on which we beat out tunes for bears to dance to, when all the time we are longing language to move the stars to pity.
Gustave Flaubert

One of the greatest sources of misunderstanding and conflict among people is the misinterpretation of the words which are used in conversation. For example, think of a time when you tried to get a message across to someone only to find that they completely misunderstood what you were saying with unwanted consequences.

From an early age we are taught to believe that language provides the clearest and most descriptive way of presenting ideas and facts. And yet our language is littered with words and phrases which mean different things to different people. We use words to describe our experiences, but of course these words are not the experiences themselves. They are simply the closest verbal approximation we can find to express ourselves.

If you were to use the word *love* in a sentence few would stop to query the meaning. However, were you to ask a hundred people to describe what love means for them, you might get a hundred different descriptions. Living in Britain we might find it relatively easy to describe the meaning of the word *snow*. However, further north, the Eskimo has many different words for snow. There is snow you can fall through, snow you can build an igloo from, snow you can eat, etc. Survival, for an Eskimo, can depend on a precise understanding of different kinds of snow.

For the teacher and manager in a school, effective communication is essential to the learning process and to the management of learning within an organisational context. An understanding of how people think and verbalise those thoughts is a vital ingredient in getting the best from people in order to bring about continuous improvement in the performance of the school.

What follows is an adaptation of a model for effective communication, the *Meta Model* developed in **"The Structure of Magic I"** (Science and Behaviour Books, 1975.) by Richard Bandler and John Grinder, the originators of Neuro-Linguistic Programming. This model can help us to understand better how we use language and how we can form a clearer picture of other people's mental maps. It is a set of skilfully formed questions which can help unlock even the most persistent barriers to effective communication.

Think for a moment of an occasion when have you been in a conversation with someone. They may have been seeking your advice or expressing a strongly held opinion. You may have paused for a moment to ask yourself *"How can I respond to this?"* or *"What is the most useful question I can ask here?"* The Meta Model helps to answer these questions. It is a useful tool for gaining a better understanding of what people mean by what they say. It can be used to unlock the subtext or underlying message in what someone is saying, and expose beliefs that they may hold about themselves and others.

The Meta Model distinguishes between the *surface structure* of any communication i.e. the actual words used and the *deeper structure* which holds the key to the thinking processes and belief systems from which the original idea is generated.

6   The Meta Model

The Meta Model is a series of questions that seek to uncover the deeper meaning of a communication which is often hidden by the words that are actually spoken. There are three main ways to obscure the true meaning of a communication.

Generalisation

Deletion

Distortion

6.1   Generalisation

This occurs when the speaker generalises from one or several experiences to a broader belief. Such generalisation restricts a person's response and his/her ability to discriminate between events and experiences. People tend to generalise in three main ways:

a.   They tend to use over-the-top generalisations known as *universals*. Common words which represent such universals in conversation include: all, always, ever, never, every, nobody, no one, everybody.

Examples   *Nobody ever pays attention to what I have to say.*
*You **always** put me down.*
*He **never** marks his pupils' books.*

Such statements are guaranteed to raise the temperature in a conversation and generate feelings of anger and resentment. In so doing they can scupper any chance of a calm and rational discussion of sensitive issues and wreck communication. To deal with such generalisations it is important to try to expose, through questioning, the weakness of the statement. This gains more specific information and uncovers the hidden thoughts and feelings.

Example	*I'll never be able to do that.*
Possible responses	*What **never**? (emphasised by tone or volume.)*
	or
	Can you remember a time when you did do it or something similar?
Outcome	**The memory of past successes can generate new possibilities.**

b.   The second form which generalisation can take is the use of *can't* or *won't* words which imply that no other choice exists for the speaker.

> *Examples*   I **won't** stand for it.
> You **can't** do that.
> That's **impossible**.

Where it is prevalent, this form of generalisation can undermine the creation of a *can do* culture which is essential for the continuous improvement of a school. It often has little to do with capability but rather reflects negative belief systems which undermine confidence, restrict creativity and prevent people from looking at situations from different angles. To deal with this form of generalisation it is important to expose the beliefs which underpin the generalisation and to rationalise the consequences of what ever action is proposed.

Example	I can't share my concerns with my head of department.
Possible responses	What exactly is stopping you from sharing your concerns with her? **or** What would happen if you did?
Outcome	**Limiting beliefs are exposed and opportunities for additional choices and alternative behaviours are created.**

c.   The third form of generalisation involves the use of *should* or *have to* words which imply fear of a higher authority, a limited view of the world, and the abdication of personal responsibility. They also indicate the existence of limiting beliefs which may well have their origin in childhood conditioning.

> *Examples*   You **shouldn't** behave like that.
> I **have to** help with the Open Evening.
> I **mustn't** be late for the senior management team meeting.

Where this form of generalisation is widely used in a school, it will most likely reflect a hierarchical structure as well as a significant sense of disempowerment among staff and pupils. In order to respond to this form of generalisation, it is vital to expose limiting beliefs and promote discussion of possible alternative courses of action.

Example	We have to do what the head says - he is the boss after all.
Possible response	What would happen if we didn't?
Outcome:	**This response enables a more rational discussion about possible effects of acting against the wishes of the head. It promotes openness to alternative courses of action.**

Avoid the use of the word "why" in response to such statements. Whilst it may elicit responses which raise important moral and ethical issues, it may not necessarily move the communication forward to a satisfactory outcome!

6.2   Deletion

Deletion occurs when information is omitted which we assume the other person understands, or we simply think is not sufficiently important to verbalise. Unfortunately, such omission can sometimes result in serious communication problems, largely because it is difficult to actually pinpoint to whom or to what a particular reference is directed.

a.   Nouns

As mentioned earlier, there are many words in our language which have different meanings for different people. There are a host of generic nouns which require clarification to avoid confusion.

For example, to say *I like fruit* requires clarification. Which particular kinds of fruit does the speaker like? Equally, to say *I don't have a good relationship with my head of department* also requires clarification. The listener needs to know more about the nature of the speaker's relationship with the head of department. In both cases further information is required.

To deal with such vague or unspecified nouns the following responses are suggested:

Example	*I need a change.*
Possible response	*What kind of change specifically do you think you need?*
Outcome	**The response enables the speaker to reveal more information about what they might like to do differently.**

Another form of noun which pervades the English language and which causes a great deal of misunderstanding is the abstract noun, also known as *nominalisation*.

Nominalisations are nouns which describe processes. They occur when a person changes a verb which is *active in time* to a noun which is *static in time.* When a verb is transformed into a noun in this way, the active process which the verb once described is lost and replaced by a vague catch-all word which has as many different meanings as the day is long! *Fear, failure, success, motivation, leadership, confusion, happiness, etc.*- the list is endless.

The problem with nominalisations is that they get in the way of effective communication. They create gaps in understanding which can be very difficult to bridge. Politicians and managers are renowned for employing nominalisations to obscure the reality of a situation! To deal with nominalisations it is important to try to change the noun back to the verb form.

Example	I'm a failure.
Possible responses	How are you failing?
	or
	In what particular area are you failing?
Outcome	**The response should reduce the generalisation of failure in everything to a specific area. It should lead to the speaker identifying a specific area of difficulty which you may then be able to address constructively.**

b.   Pronouns

The second form of deletion is when the speaker does not specify whom or what they are talking about. This is caused by the use of vague pronouns such as *they, him, she, it, those, this, others.*

Example	They all look down on me.
Possible response	Who specifically looks down on you?
Outcome	**This response personalises this issue and can lead to a more focused discussion about the perceived problem.**

c.   Verbs

Verbs can also be misleading, particularly when they give insufficient information about the specifics of the process they describe. The surface structure of the verb may obscure the deeper structure of the message.

Example	She undermined my position.
Possible responses	In what way did she undermine your position?
	or
	What exactly did she do which undermined your position?
Outcome	**The deeper structure of the communication is revealed and you gain a valuable insight into the other person's "map".**

d. Adjectives

The vague use of adjectives can also cause information to be deleted.

Example	*I am unhappy.*
Possible responses	*What or whom exactly are you unhappy about.* *or* *How specifically are you making yourself unhappy?*
Outcome	**Once again, the deeper structure of the communication is revealed and omitted information is uncovered.**

e. Comparisons

The final form of deletion occurs when someone makes unspecified *comparisons*. Common words in this category include: *better, worse, best, worst.* In each case what is omitted is the benchmark against which the value judgement can be made.

Example	*She is a better teacher.*
Possible responses	*Compared with whom?* *or* *In what way is she a better teacher?*
Outcome	**These responses will reveal the invalidity of the comparison or will stimulate a discussion of the criteria against which the comparisons are made.**

6.3. Distortion

The distortion of language, either intentionally or unwittingly, often serves to obscure the true meaning of a statement and so impedes effective communication. Distortion takes a number of different forms including *presupposition, mind reading, the equating of one experience with another, value judgements and the creation of cause and effect links between two experiences.* The ability to recognise and respond effectively to distortion patterns is a valuable linguistic skill which helps cut through much of the *fluff* which blocks the satisfactory resolution of interpersonal difficulties.

a. Presuppositions

Presuppositions arise when the speaker makes assumptions about the conditions which must exist before something can or cannot happen.

Example	*I can't take on this extra responsibility effectively because I love my teaching.*
Possible response	*How does your loving teaching mean that you are not able to take on this extra responsibility?*
Outcome	**This response exposes the assumption that one cannot carry extra responsibilities as well as teach effectively. Once this assumption is exposed a more open discussion of the possibilities for marrying the two roles successfully can follow.**

b.   **Mind Reading**

Mind reading occurs when one person assumes they know how another person thinks and feels. Sometimes we mind read intuitively by reading a person's body language. Often we are simply projecting our own thoughts and feelings onto another. Occasionally, mind reading is used as a weapon in an interpersonal dispute. Whatever form it takes, mind reading is a pattern which can be exposed by eliciting from someone the evidence on which they have based their statement.

Example	*You're not listening to me.*
Possible responses	*How exactly do you know I am not listening to you?* *or* *What leads you to believe that?*
Outcome	**Either of these responses uncovers the sensory evidence which lead the person to arrive at his conclusion and allows the subject to agree with, or dispute, the statement.**

c.   **Equation**

The equation of one experience with another is a common form of language distortion. Commonly, two statements are set alongside each other to give the impression that they mean the same thing. It is often simply a case of jumping to conclusions, rightly or wrongly. However, the use of such patterns injects unnecessary emotion into an interaction whilst at the same time masking the real meaning of the communication. Once this pattern has been identified it is important to separate the two statements to have a chance of accessing the real meaning.

Example	*The head has just cut the time allocation for Music - he's a philistine.*
Possible response	*How does his cutting of the time allocation for Music mean that he is a philistine?*
Outcome	**Such a response can break the link between the two statements, de-personalise the issue and allow a dispassionate discussion of the situation.**

d. Value Judgements

People frequently make value judgements in conversation. More often than not such judgements appear to have neither source nor clear criteria. Television advertisements are typically based around value judgements. *It's good to talk* and *Probably the best lager in the world.*

To respond to such value judgements we need to identify the source of the value judgement and the criteria on which it is based.

Example	*Progressive teaching methods lower standards.*
Possible response	*How do you know progressive teaching methods lower standards?* *or* *Who is making this judgement and on what basis?*
Outcome	**The author of the statement is challenged to validate the claims implied in the judgement.**

e. Cause and Effect Relationship between two Experiences

The final form of distortion occurs when a person establishes a cause and effect relationship between two experiences. For example, in the statement, *Her singing drives me mad* the speaker is associating feelings of anger and irritation with the singing voice of another, as if the singer had a direct control over the speaker's thoughts and feelings.

The word *but* can provide clues to the use of the cause and effect pattern. *I would have told you **but** I thought you would be angry with me.*

The belief that one's emotional state can be determined by the actions of others is very limiting. Therefore, it is important to expose the limitations of the assumed causal link to ensure that the locus of control remains firmly with oneself.

Example	*The deputy head's superior attitude really annoys me.*
Possible response	*How does his superior attitude annoy you?* *or* *How are you annoying yourself with his attitude?*
Outcome	**These questions reveal the nature of the perceived causal link and allows the speaker to focus attention on his or her own responsibility in the situation.**

The Meta Model will repay regular practice. The ability to spot specific language patterns and the skilled use of key questions - such as those above - to unlock the underpinning beliefs, will improve the effectiveness of your interpersonal communication. It will enable you in your managerial role to quickly get to the heart of issues and problems by developing clarity of thinking. It will improve your ability to *think on your feet* and it will improve listening skills. Most importantly, if used in conjunction with *rapport skills* and *congruence*, it will prove to be a worthwhile investment in terms of getting to know better how colleagues, pupils and parents think and feel.

Section Six

Resolving Differences Effectively

In this section you will learn about:

☛ **How to conduct negotiations in a principled way to achieve win/win outcomes.**

☛ **An approach to mediating successfully in disputes between parties.**

☛ **Techniques for dealing with difficult people.**

In the long history of humankind (and animalkind too) those who learn to collaborate most effectively have prevailed.

Charles Darwin

1   Principled Negotiation

Negotiation is a natural feature of human interaction. We negotiate all the time. Whether we are bartering for a reduction in price, or deciding how to spend our family holidays, we are continually seeking to resolve differences of choice or opinion in a way which leaves everyone feeling satisfied with the outcome. Much of the day-to-day work of a manager in a school involves negotiating with pupils, parents, senior managers, suppliers, etc. Much of this work is conducted affably, with little stress, and is simply perceived as part of the job.

However, when the subject of negotiation is introduced in a formal sense - e.g. negotiating for your department's share of capitation or curriculum time - then for many school managers what springs to mind is argument, position-taking, demands and counter-demands, all surrounded by an accompanying element of stress! A classic case of negative reframing.

It need not be so. The ability to negotiate sensitively and effectively is the key to creating the kind of culture of openness and trust in a school that is essential to continuous improvement.

Ursula Markham in her book **"Managing Conflict"** (Thorsons, 1996) defines negotiation as:

A method of discussion and interaction which enables two or more parties, each with their own aims and desired outcomes, to come together to a satisfactory conclusion - one which is to everyone's advantage. The outcome of a successful negotiation is a win/win situation which results in all parties being content. It does not involve one party or group of people taking unfair advantage of the other or using devious methods because they are determined to get their own way no matter who else suffers in the process.

This definition describes what is sometimes known as *principled negotiation* in which both parties operate with integrity to achieve a mutually satisfactory outcome.

Principled negotiation recognises that, because there is a difference of opinion between the parties involved, negotiation only occurs if one or both of the parties are prepared to budge from their position to some extent or other. This understanding of the need for some degree of give and take, if not by the other party then by you, is crucial to the successful outcome of any negotiation.

Principled negotiation also assumes that whatever outcome is agreed, it will be adopted in practice by *both parties*. In principled negotiation there is no place for the social chameleon who says one thing then does another. An agreement means very little if it is not sustained by character and relationship.

In a school it is important to approach *win/win* negotiations from a genuine desire to invest in the relationships that make such outcomes possible.

A negotiated agreement can occur in response to a number of different approaches:

Splitting the Difference	The basis of this approach is to meet somewhere in the middle, to compromise in order to avoid conflict. Splitting the difference can be quick and simple. It may not necessarily lead to the most effective solution to a problem but rather to a 'fudge', which in the long term, pleases no one.
Bartering	Bartering is about exchanging things of value to each party. Both parties trade negotiating points with each other in a process of give and take. Exchanges are often of different types of concessions. The pitfalls of this approach lie in the fact that what is exchanged may not actually have equivalent values. This can lead to dissatisfaction on the part of one or other parties and a feeling of having been cheated in some form or other.
Power Play	Power Play occurs when one party uses their dominant position to influence the other party to generate a settlement which is favourable to themselves. Power Play may bring short term acquiescence but ultimately leads to resentment and disaffection.
Emotional Blackmail	The use of emotion is a powerful, though not necessarily helpful, tool in negotiation. A carefully timed display of anger, disappointment, tears or even laughter can often sway the outcomes of a negotiation, although not necessarily towards the most appropriate solution. It can obscure the real issues and leave one or other of the parties feeling that they have been manipulated.
Reasoned Argument	The careful construction of a reasoned argument, backed by clear evidence, can often be persuasive enough to bring about a negotiated agreement. It requires careful planning and may need to allow time for the parties to reflect on the evidence and to prepare counter arguments.

Improving Personal Effectiveness for Managers in Schools

2   Conducting Win/Win Negotiations

It is important to be alert to the strengths and pitfalls of the various factors which influence the outcome of a negotiation and to respond assertively to any hint of manipulation. Having said that, the following procedure for the conduct of negotiations is designed to achieve mutually agreed outcomes in a principled and structured way.

The Negotiation Process

Step 1   Planning for the Negotiation Process

Before you enter a negotiation it is important to take some preliminary steps.

1. First, clarify what it is you really want to achieve from the negotiation. What would be, for you, the most satisfying result?

2. Secondly, establish what would be your *bottom line* and how far you might be prepared to move. This is what is known as your BATNA or *best alternative to a negotiated agreement.*

3. Be clear about what is for discussion - and what is not for discussion - or you may get side-tracked into irrelevant issues.

4. Make sure you have to hand all relevant documentation.

5. Think about anything specific that you can offer the other party to encourage movement from their position.

Step 2   Negotiation in Action

There are some general guidelines for the conduct of negotiations.

1. It is important to separate the people from the problems. Getting embroiled in moral or character issues is a shortcut to stalemate.

2. It is more constructive to focus attention on the *interests* of the different parties rather than on the positions they and you might assume.

3. It is important to explore a number of different possible solutions before coming to a final agreement.

4. It is also helpful that any agreement reached is based on some objective criteria which all the parties agree to be fair.

In addition...

● Enter any negotiation with a positive outlook. You are not going to war! The aim is to arrive at a mutually agreed solution - not to get bogged down in petty wrangling. One-upmanship has no place in principled negotiation.

- Reinforce this approach by building rapport with the other party. Rapport is the lubrication which enables the discussions to flow more freely.

- Stay calm, listen attentively to what the other party has to say. Don't be drawn into arguments. Take time to consider what they are saying. Don't mind read or make hasty judgements about what they are saying.

- Speak slowly and clearly, checking that they fully understand what you have to say. Make it clear at the outset that your aim is to arrive at a mutually agreeable solution.

- Be congruent in everything you say and do to build trust and confidence. Remember to look for signs of congruence or incongruence in the other party.

- Be flexible and open to alternatives you might not have considered. Use your knowledge of perceptual positions to see the situation from first, second and third positions. Use the Meta Model to question statements and detect hidden agendas and limiting beliefs that might block the way to a satisfactory solution.

- Remember your boundaries and limits. Be assertive and ready to say "No" if the discussion enters territory where you feel you are not prepared to compromise.

- When you reach agreement make sure that both parties fully understand the implications and agree appropriate actions and time scales.

Step 3   After the Negotiation

- Follow up the verbal agreement with a written note listing the outcomes of the discussion and the relevant actions and time scales to be circulated to all relevant parties for comment.

- Carry out agreed actions and establish a mechanism for receiving feedback from the other party.

- Review the outcomes of the agreement at an appropriate time.

3   Mediating the Differences of Others

There may be times as a school manager - e.g. in a dispute between a teacher and a pupil or between two colleagues - when you are called upon to act as a mediator, with the task of helping others to resolve their differences.

Managers have much to lose in such situations. If one or both of the parties feel that you have acted unfairly in favour of the other, your intervention may rebound on you and result in future problems, resentment and disaffection. On the other hand, the ability to demonstrate integrity and skill in bringing about a successful *win/win* resolution to the differences of others can enhance your status as a leader and manager. It can also promote the culture of openness and trust that is so essential for effective school leadership and management.

Before we concentrate on the process of mediation, remember that the outcome of mediation may not always be compromise. There will be situations where one of the parties is indisputably at fault. Perhaps they have clearly breached some school policy or guidelines, or they are acting in a manner which places pupils at risk. Where, for example, a teacher is regularly turning up late for lessons and so causing another colleague to be late for their lessons, then discipline rather than compromise is required. As a manager you have to make those distinctions!

In other circumstances, however, differing values and belief systems or behaviour patterns may result in differences of opinion between two people in relation to a particular issue. In such cases a structured process of mediation can help to resolve differences.

The Mediation Process

Step 1   The Arrangements

● Arrange a meeting in a neutral location and invite the parties concerned. Choose an appropriate time of day and allow sufficient time for the meeting. (A hurried lunch time meeting is not a good idea!)

● Declare the purposes of the meeting at the outset to enable both parties to muster their arguments and gather evidence if appropriate. (There should be no unexpected traps.)

● Ensure that the meeting place is conducive to the conduct of confidential, interpersonal discussions. Put both parties at their ease to help build rapport.

● Make the necessary arrangements to make sure that the meeting is not interrupted.

Step 2   The Start of the Meeting

● Sit between the two parties. Break the ice with some general conversation. Seek to build rapport with both parties and to establish your neutrality.

● From your own perspective, articulate the problem that lies between the parties as best as you can.

● Establish the desired outcome of the meeting and clarify the process and your role. (Remember - you are a facilitator not a judge!)

- Discuss and agree ground rules: each to speak in turn; the other to listen without interruption; no raised voices or personal attacks; focus on behaviour not personality.

- Use positive language. Focus on the positive consequences of resolving the problem for both parties and for the school.

Step 3   The Core of the Meeting

- Each party, in turn and without interruption, describes the problem and its causes as they see it.

- Each party describes what they would see as the most acceptable outcome to the problem.

- As facilitator, "chunk up" both sides of the argument until both parties can agree on a higher level outcome. For example, despite their differences over the particular issue, both parties might eventually agree that what is most important is the well-being of the pupils in the school. Once you have this point of agreement you can then gradually "chunk down" until agreement is reached on a lower level outcome.

- Ask both parties in turn to identify what they would be prepared to concede in order to help find a resolution to their differences.

- Backtrack regularly to clarify and summarise what each party is saying.

- Remain in rapport. Do not allow yourself to be drawn into the arguments.

- Keep the discussion on track and be assertive in coming down on red herrings or the use of derogatory remarks.

- Continue back and forth until agreement is reached.

Step 4   Concluding the Meeting

- Summarise the discussion, giving equal weight to the views of both parties.

- Clarify the outcomes and agreed actions.

- Seek a congruent response from each party that they are willing to accept the agreed outcomes. If either party appears hesitant or incongruent, then continue to explore their concerns until both parties are clearly satisfied with the outcome.

> **Step 5   After the Meeting**
>
> ● Summarise the agreed outcomes and send a written record of the agreed outcomes to each party.
>
> ● Check at an appropriate time on the progress of the agreement.

4.   Red Herrings and Dead Ends

As the facilitator of the mediation process, it is important that you are alert to the two most common obstacles to the resolution of differences: *red herrings* and *dead ends*. Red herrings occur when irrelevant or anecdotal information is brought into the conversation by either party. These red herrings divert the discussion away from the main issues. Red herrings waste time and energy, cause irritation and hijack the mediation process.

As facilitator you must spot red herrings and stop them in their tracks with the simple challenge:

> **Forgive me for interrupting, but I'm not clear how your talking about 'x' is helping us to achieve 'y' .**

A dead-end occurs when one or other of the parties comes up with a statement such as *Well that's it, I can't see a way out of this!* or *There's no point in going on*. Statements like these are simply attempts to block the process. Challenge them with the question:

> **So what would have to happen for us to be able to...?**

However, what is often surprising about the process of mediation, is the way it frequently reveals how much the parties have in common, so helping to undermine what divides them. Conducted in a structured way, in a spirit of rapport throughout, the process of mediation helps to strengthen relationships by placing petty differences in the wider context of shared values and goals.

5   Dealing with Difficult People

There has been a great deal of change in our schools in the past ten years. Accompanying that change has been greater parental involvement, an enhanced role for governors, and intense political and media interest in standards in schools. Continuing financial constraint has resulted in larger class sizes, increased workload and fewer career opportunities.

Many people working in schools have adapted well to these changes, but for others, as in any organisation, change has been painful and difficult. Teacher morale has been badly affected and some teachers have found it difficult to retain the kind of enthusiasm for the job which first brought them into teaching. Needless to say, some teachers have reacted to that by becoming disillusioned, and by exhibiting what might be described as problem behaviour and underperformance.

Dealing with the interpersonal problems of colleagues, as well as pupils and parents, has become an integral and challenging part of the school manager's job in recent years. The inability to deal effectively and assertively with so called difficult people causes more stomach-knotting stress and feelings of inadequacy among school managers, from headteachers to curriculum co-ordinators, than any other aspect of the role. Ask yourself a few simple questions to gauge your response to conflict situations.

When dealing with someone who can be difficult or obstructive which of the following do you tend to do:

1. Respond in a hostile manner and take up a counter position to theirs.

2. Speak assertively to persuade them to behave more constructively.

3. Listen carefully to what they have to say and try to see things from their point of view.

4. Walk away in anger when you are confronted by them.

5. Try to avoid them altogether.

6. Worry about what you are going to say when you meet them.

The discipline of Neuro-Linguistic Programming offers an interesting perspective on the problem of difficult people. A key operating principle of NLP is that everyone acts with a positive intention. However difficult their behaviour may seem, they are probably trying to achieve something of value for themselves.

Sometimes, of course, it is not always easy to fathom what the positive intention is in the behaviour of a person who is constantly obstructive and negative in outlook. How they behave can seem bizarre or annoying. We are all different and see the world in different ways. Consequently we do not always really know what others are trying to achieve. We do not see their actions from their point of view unless we use our knowledge of perceptual positions.

In the same way, others may not see our actions from our point of view. Their understanding can be very different from our intention. Remember the principle, *the meaning of your communication is the response it gets.* This is a way of saying: *Look at your actions and words from the other person's point of view as well as your own.*

It can be difficult to change someone's behaviour without first changing your own. The following process provides a way of dealing with situations in which the recurring behaviour of another person causes you problems.

On first reading you may find the procedures a little unusual. However, they will give you a real insight into not only the motivation of the other person but also into your own motivation.

Step 1   Identify the person with whom you have an ongoing difficulty.

Step 2   Try to identify a specific situation that has happened a number of times in the past and is likely to happen in the future.

Step 3   Make sure that you are comfortable with addressing this issue. If you are not, ask yourself why not? Only proceed when you are happy to explore this issue.

Step 4   Using your knowledge of perceptual positions, set up geographical locations for first, second and third positions in a room. (See diagram). As a rule of thumb, third position should be twice as far away as first is from second position. Third position, for the purpose of this process, is that of an observer from which you can watch the behaviours of the other people from a safe position. To accentuate this, you might like to imagine that there is a two way mirror separating third position from the other two positions.

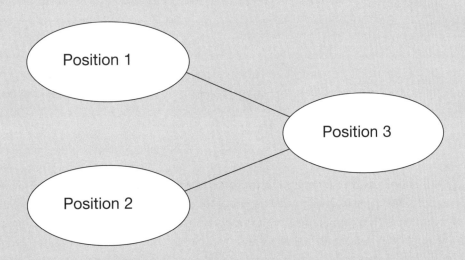

Step 5   Now step into third position. From this position notice the behaviours of the people in first and second positions. Describe the behaviours of each with an adjective (e.g. defensive, angry, etc.) Use words like *he, she, they* to describe what is happening between the first and second persons.

Step 6   Step out of third position and move to first position. In first position notice what is happening for you. Seeing the situation through your own eyes, notice your thoughts, feelings, beliefs, and any sights and sounds as you look at the person in second position. What is your positive intention in thinking and feeling as you do about the person in second position? What would your positive intention get you? Use words like *I, me, us.*

Step 7   Now step out of first position. Take a moment to shake of the associated thoughts and feelings.

Return to third position and notice anything new in the way you perceive what is happening between the two other persons now that you have more information about the situation.

Step 8   Now move to second position and try to step inside the shoes of the person with whom you are having difficulties. Try to adopt their facial expressions and mannerisms. Imagine what is going on for you (them). If in doubt simply guess! Describe your thoughts and feelings and beliefs about the situation for yourself and that person in the other chair. What is your positive intention and what would that get for you?

Step 9   Move out of second position and return to third position and once again notice any differences in the way you feel about the situation. Establish what the person in first position could do differently now they have a different understanding of the situation. Generate ideas for new and different behaviour that the person in first position might be happy to execute.

Step 10   Go back to first position and ask yourself, "Can I do this behaviour?" If yes, try to imagine the next time you encounter the other person and try in your imagination to see if you could demonstrate this new behaviour?

With thanks to John Seymour for this material.

What this process can give you is a different insight into the nature of your relationship with the other person. It can provide you with choices in how you behave towards the person. Whilst it might confirm your views about the obduracy of the other person, it might just help you break out of a relationship loop into which you may be as firmly hooked as the person who is presenting the difficulties. You might even find that you have become part of the problem!

Remember - the person with the greatest flexibility of thought and action usually has the greatest influence on the outcome of an interaction.

6   Addressing Underperformance With Sensitivity

Having said that, there are times when it is necessary to criticise aspects of the work of others. How such criticism is handled is a key factor in whether it brings about desired improvement in performance or not. In his book **"Emotional Intelligence"** *(Bloomsbury, 1996)* Daniel Goleman provides advice on what he describes as the *artful critique*. This focuses on what a person has done and can do, rather than assuming character deficiencies because of a job poorly done.

Goleman suggests that attacking someone's character either intentionally or not - e.g. calling someone stupid or incompetent - misses the point. When you appear to be attacking the person, rather than their behaviour, you immediately put them on the defensive, so that he or she is no longer receptive to what you have to tell him about how to do things better.

In terms of motivation, when someone believes that their failures are due to some unchangeable deficit in themselves, they lose hope and stop trying.

The basic principles which should pervade any school is that there are:

No failures - only feedback. No mistakes - only results .

The following guidelines on the art of the critique, developed by Harry Levinson and referred to in **"Emotional Intelligence"**, provide useful advice to managers on how to improve the performance of colleagues:

The Skill of the Artful Critique

Stage 1.　　Be specific

● Choose a particular aspect or incident that illustrates shortcomings in the work of the other person.

● Focus on the specific actions and/or behaviours which the person has exhibited in this particular situation.

● Describe as specifically as possible what went well, what was done badly, and how it could be changed.

Stage 2.　　Offer a solution

● Discuss specific ways of improving the situation. This might open up new possibilities and alternatives for the other person.

● Discuss the needs of the person in addressing the issue and making the necessary changes to their behaviour.

Stage 3.　　Be Present

● Deal with the giving of constructive criticism face to face.

● Avoid sending memos which can be impersonal, generate resentment and rob the person of opportunities for response or clarification.

Stage 4.　　Be Sensitive

● Build rapport to gain a better understanding of the impact of what you are saying on the other person - this is the skill of empathy.

● Avoid the withering put down which can be destructive and counterproductive.

In recent years there has been an increasing emphasis on mechanistic approaches to the evaluation of the work of schools eg. target setting, league tables, the use of performance data and Ofsted inspections. It is all too easy to forget that at the core of the educational process and the work of schools are the myriad of interactions which take place on a daily basis between teachers, parents and pupils. It is the quality of these interactions, rather than any statistical analysis - however sophisticated - which is fundamental to the success of the teaching and learning process.

The emphasis which the leaders and managers of a school place on ensuring that all members of the school community feel valued and supported can go some way towards explaining the difference in ethos and performance between apparently similar schools. A recognition that every individual brings to their school experience their own particular map of the world is an important starting point in creating a positive and constructive ethos in a school. In dealing with difficulties when they arise, the use of win/win approaches, such as those described in this section, which recognise and value individual points of view, could be the approaches that make the difference.

Conclusion

It is encouraging to read the specifications for the National Professional Qualification for Headteachers, the new national standards for subject leaders and indeed the Leadership Programme for Serving Headteachers, all recently launched by the Teacher Training Agency. Alongside the obvious focus on the development of technical managerial competencies, there is a refreshing recognition of the important role of managers in schools in leading and motivating the staff with whom they work.

In attempting to motivate others, an effective leader will begin by articulating the vision for a school. This vision will need to reflect the shared goals and values of other staff if he or she hopes to move others forward. Leaders motivate people by taking the time and making the effort to find out what is important to them. Only by investing in people and by applying the kinds of skills described in this book can the school manager embody the necessary personal, interpersonal and organisational values.

The presupposition of this book is that to lead others you must first be capable of leading yourself. The ability to build rapport with - and between - others and to create a school or departmental ethos in which colleagues value and support each other, is a factor of self belief and explicit role modelling. For it is clear that unless you believe in what you are doing and act in accordance with those beliefs, few will join you and the task of meeting your avowed objectives will be all the more complex and difficult. If the material in this book has helped you to appreciate this fundamental principle and has encouraged you to begin the journey towards greater self awareness and improved personal effectiveness, then it will have served its main purpose.

If some of the processes described in the book have seemed a little unusual, it is because they are adapted from training activities. The live and shared experiences of a recognised programme of personal development training, such as those mentioned in the further reading section of this book, provides the most effective vehicle for learning and practising the skills which will improve your personal and interpersonal effectiveness.

Suggestions for Further Reading

Adair, John   **Effective Leadership** (Gower, 1983)

Adler, Dr. Harry   **NLP for Managers** (Piatkus, 1996)

Andreas, Steve and Connirae   **Heart of the Mind** (Real People Press, 1990)

Andreas, Steve and Connirae   **Change Your Mind - and Keep the Change** (Real People Press, 1987)

Bandler, Richard   **Using Your Brain for a Change** (Real People Press, 1985)

Bandler, Richard and Grinder,John   **into Princes** (Real People Press, 1979)

Bandler, Richard and Grinder,John   **Reframing** (Real People Press, 1982)

Bandler, Richard and Grinder,John   **The Structure of Magic 1** (Science and Behaviour Books, 1975)

Berne, Eric   **Games People Play** (Penguin, 1964)

Charvet, Shelle Rose   **Words that Change Minds** (Kendall Hunt, 1995)

Covey, Stephen   **Seven Habits of Highly Effective People** (Simon and Schuster, 1989)

Covey, Stephen   **Principled Centred Leadership** (Simon and Schuster, 1992)

DfEE   **Excellence in School** (The Stationery Office Ltd, 1997)

Dilts, Robert   **Changing Belief Systems with NLP** (Meta Publications, 1990)

Drummond, Helga   **Managing Difficult Staff** (Kogan Page, 1990)

Fisher, Roger and Ury, William   **Getting to Yes** (Business Books, 1997)

Gelb, Michael J. and Buzan, Tony   **Lessons from the Art of Juggling** (Aurum Press, 1995)

Goleman, Daniel   **Emotional Intelligence** (Bloomsbury, 1996)

Hagemann, Gisela   **The Motivational Manual** (Gower, 1992)

Hall, L. Michael — **The Spirit of NLP** (Anglo American Book Company, 1996)

Harris, Thomas A. — **I'm OK - You're OK** (Pan Books, 1973)

Kindler, Herbert S. — **Managing Disagreement Constructively** (Crisp Publications Inc., 1988)

Laborde, Genie — **Influencing with Integrity** (Syntony Publishing Company, 1984)

Markham, Ursula — **Managing Conflict** (Thorsons, 1996)

Markham, Ursula — **How to Deal with Difficult People** (Thorsons, 1993)

McDermott, Ian and O'Connor, Joseph — **Practical NLP for Managers** (Gower, 1996)

O'Connor, Joseph and Seymour, John — **Introducing NLP** (Harper Collins, 1990)

Richardson, J. and Margoulis, J. — **The Magic of Rapport** (Meta Publications, 1988)

Robbins, Anthony — **Unlimited Power** (Simon and Schuster, 1988)

Robbins, Anthony — **Awaken the Giant Within** (Simon and Schuster, 1991)

Smith, Manuel J. — **When I Say No, I Feel Guilty** (Bantam Books, 1975)

Turner, Colin and Andrews, Phillippa — **One to One Interpersonal Skills for Managers** (Staff College, 1994)

Turner, Colin — **Born to Succeed (**Element, 1994)

Training

Neuro-linguistic Programming has influenced much of this book.
For more information contact.

John Seymour Associates
17 Boyce Drive
St. Werburghs
Bristol BS2 9XQ
Tel: 0117 955 7827
email: jsa@netgates.co.uk

"Improving Personal Effectiveness for Managers in Schools" is the eleventh title in *The School Effectiveness Series*, which focuses on practical and useful ideas for individual schools and teachers. This series addresses the issues of whole school improvement along with new knowledge about teaching and learning, and offers straightforward solutions which teachers can use to make life more rewarding for themselves and those they teach.

Book 1: *Accelerated Learning in the Classroom* by Alistair Smith
ISBN: 1-85539-034-5   £15.95
- The first book in the UK to apply new knowledge about the brain to classroom practice
- Contains practical methods so teachers can apply accelerated learning theories to their own classrooms
- Aims to increase the pace of learning and deepen understanding
- Includes advice on how to create the ideal enviroment for learning and how to help learners fulfil their potential
- Offers practical solutions on improving performance, motivation and understanding

Book 2: *Effective Learning Activities* by Chris Dickinson
ISBN: 1-85539-035-3   £8.95
- An essential teaching guide which focuses on practical activities to improve learning
- Aims to improve results through effective learning, which will raise achievement, deepen understanding, promote self-esteem and improve motivation
- Includes activities which are designed to promote differentiation and understanding
- Includes activities suitable for GCSE, National Curriculum, Highers, GSVQ and GNVQ

Book 3: *Effective Heads of Department* by Phil Jones & Nick Sparks
ISBN: 1-85539-036-1   £8.95
- Contains a range of practical systems and approaches; each of the eight sections ends with a 'checklist for action'
- Designed to develop practice in line with OFSTED expectations and DfEE thinking by monitoring and improving quality
- Addresses issues such as managing resources, leadership, learning, departmental planning and making assessment valuable
- Includes useful information for senior managers in schools who are looking to enhance the effectiveness of their Heads of Department

Book 4: *Lessons are for Learning* by Mike Hughes
ISBN: 1-85539-038-8   £11.95
- Brings together the theory of learning with the realities of the classroom environment
- Encourages teachers to reflect on their own classroom practice and challenges them to think about why they teach in the way they do
- Offers practical suggestions for activities that bridge the gap between recent developments in the theory of learning and the constraints in classroom teaching
- Ideal for stimulating thought and generating discussion

Book 5: *Effective Learning in Science* by Paul Denley and Keith Bishop
ISBN: 1-85539-039-6   £11.95
- Encourages discussion about the aims and purposes in teaching science and the role of subject knowledge in effective teaching
- Tackles issues such as planning for effective learning, the use of resources and other relevant management issues
- Offers help in the development of a departmental plan to revise schemes of work, resources, classroom strategies, in order to make learning and teaching more effective
- Ideal for any science department aiming to increase performance and improve results

Book 6: *Raising Boys' Achievement* by Jon Pickering

ISBN: 1-85539-040-X   £11.95

- Addresses the causes of boys' underachievement and offers possible solutions
- Focuses the search for causes and solutions on teachers working in the classroom
- Looks at examples of good practice in schools to help guide the planning and implementation of strategies to raise achievement
- Offers practical, 'real' solutions, along with tried and tested training suggestions
- Ideal as a basis for INSET or as a guide to practical activities for classroom teachers

Book 7: *Effective Provision for Able & Talented Children* by Barry Teare

ISBN: 1-85539-041-8   £11.95

- Basic theory, necessary procedures and turning theory into practice
- Main methods of identifying the able and talented
- Concerns about achievement and appropriate strategies to raise achievement
- The role of the classroom teacher, monitoring and evaluation techniques
- Practical enrichment activities and appropriate resources

Book 8: *Effective Careers Education & Guidance* by Andrew Edwards and Anthony Barnes

ISBN: 1-85539-045-0   £11.95

- Strategic planning of the careers programme as part of the wider curriculum
- Practical consideration of managing careers education and guidance
- Practical activities for reflection and personal learning, and case studies where such activities have been used
- Aspects of guidance and counselling involved in helping students to understand their own capabilities and form career plans
- Strategies for reviewing and developing existing practice

Book 9: *Best behaviour and Best behaviour FIRST AID* by Peter Relf, Rod Hirst,
Jan Richardson and GeorginaYoudell

ISBN: 1-85539-046-9   £12.95

- Provides support for those who seek starting points for effective behaviour management, for individual teachers and for middle and senior managers
- Focuses on practical and useful ideas for individual schools and teachers

Best behaviour FIRST AID

ISBN: 1-85539-047-7   £10.50 (pack of 5 booklets)

- Provides strategies to cope with aggression, defiance and disturbance
- Straightforward action points for self-esteem

Book 10: *The Effective School Governor* by David Marriott

ISBN 1-85539-042-6   £15.95 (including free audio tape)

- Straightforward guidance on how to fulfil a governor's role and responsibilities
- Develops your personal effectiveness as an individual governor
- Practical support on how to be an effective member of the governing team
- Audio tape for use in car or at home

Other Publications

Accelerated Learning in Practice by Alistair Smith

ISBN: 1-85539-048-5   £19.95

- The author's second book which takes Nobel Prize winning brain research into the classroom.
- Structured to help readers access and retain the information necessary to begin to accelerate their own learning and that of the students they teach.
- Contains over 100 learning tools, case studies from 36 schools and an up to the minute section.
- Includes 9 principles of learning based on brain research and the author's 7 Stage Accelerated Learning cycle.

Primary Publications

Imagine That... by Stephen Bowkett

ISBN: 1-85539-043-4   £19.95

- Hands-on, user-friendly manual for stimulating creative thinking, talking and writing in the classroom
- Provides over 100 practical and immediately useable classroom activities and games that can be used in isolation, or in combination, to help meet the requirements and standards of the National Curriculum
- Explores the nature of creative thinking and how this can be effectively driven through an ethos of positive encouragement, mutual support and celebration of success and achievement
- Empowers children to learn how to learn

Helping With Reading by Anne Butterworth and Angela White

ISBN: 1-85539-044-2   £14.95

- Includes sections on 'Hearing Children Read', 'Word Recognition' and 'Phonics'
- Provides precisely focused, easily implemented follow-up activities for pupils who need extra reinforcement of basic reading skills
- Activities which directly relate to the National Curriculum and 'Literacy Hour' group work. They are clear, practical and easily implemented. Ideas and activities can also be incorporated into Individual Education Plans
- Aims to address current concerns about reading standards and to provide support in view of the growing use of classroom assistants and parents to help with the teaching of reading